Mastering Apache Camel

An advanced guide to Enterprise Integration
using Apache Camel

Jean-Baptiste Onofré

BIRMINGHAM - MUMBAI

Mastering Apache Camel

First published: June 2015

Production reference: 1250615

Published by Packt Publishing Ltd.
Livery Place
35 Livery Street
Birmingham B3 2PB, UK.

ISBN 978-1-78217-315-1

www.packtpub.com

Credits

Author
Jean-Baptiste Onofré

Reviewers
Volker Kueffel

Carsten Ringe

Phil Wilkins

Commissioning Editor
Amarabha Banerjee

Acquisition Editor
Meeta Rajani

Content Development Editor
Anand Singh

Technical Editors
Namrata Patil

Deepti Tuscano

Copy Editors
Merilyn Pereira

Laxmi Subramanian

Project Coordinator
Vijay Kushlani

Proofreader
Safis Editing

Indexer
Rekha Nair

Production Coordinator
Melwyn D'sa

Cover Work
Melwyn D'sa

About the Author

Jean-Baptiste Onofré is a member of the Apache Software Foundation, and he has been involved in Apache projects for about 10 years. He's the PMC chair of Apache Karaf and its subprojects, including Cellar, Cave, and EIK.

He's also a PMC member of Apache ACE, Apache ServiceMix, and Apache Syncope, and he is a committer for Apache ActiveMQ, Apache Archiva, Apache Aries, Apache Camel, and Apache jClouds.

He's currently working at Talend (http://www.talend.com) as a software architect and is a member of the Talend Apache team.

He has provided articles on Java technologies for GNU/Linux magazine France and has worked as an author and a reviewer on different books, such as *Learning Karaf Cellar* and *Apache Karaf Cookbook,* both by Packt Publishing.

He has also given talks on Apache projects, such as Karaf and Camel, at different conferences, especially ApacheCon NA and Europe, CamelOne, and so on.

I would like to thank the whole Camel and Karaf team, especially Guillaume Nodet, Achim Nierbeck, Jamie Goodyear, Ioannis Canellos, Claus Ibsen, and all the others. We are a great team, and you do a great job.

I would also like to thank my wife, Lucile, who accepted that I spent some nights on this book.

About the Reviewers

Volker Kueffel has been a software engineer and architect for almost two decades and has been developing software since he was a teenager. A physicist by trade, he has worked on large-scale data systems in various verticals of the software industry, spanning from online travel, mobile, and enterprise applications to online advertising. He introduced Apache Camel into one of his projects where it has successfully served as a major system component for several years. Volker is a native of Germany and currently lives with his family in San Francisco, California.

Carsten Ringe is a software developer by heart and has been working in different industries, from defense to agriculture and logistics, in the last 10 years. Over the last couple of years, he has spent his time with Apache Camel building a scalable integration platform for a large logistics enterprise.

Phil Wilkins has spent over 25 years in the software industry, working for both multinationals and software startups. He started out as a developer and has worked his way up through technical and development leadership roles, primarily in Java-based environments. He now works as an enterprise technical architect within the IT group for a global optical healthcare manufacturer and retailer using Oracle Middleware, Cloud and RedHat JBoss technologies.

Outside of his work commitments, he has contributed his technical capabilities to supporting others in a wide range of activities from the development of community websites, to providing input and support to people authoring books and developing software ideas and businesses, including reviewing a range of technical books for Packt and other publishers. He is also a blogger and a participant in the Oracle middleware community.

When not immersed in work and technology, he spends his time pursuing his passion for music and with his wife and two boys.

I'd like to take this opportunity to thank my wife, Catherine, and our two sons, Christopher and Aaron, for their tolerance and for the innumerable hours that I've spent in front of a computer, contributing to activities for both, my employer and many other IT-related activities that I've supported over the years.

www.PacktPub.com

Support files, eBooks, discount offers, and more

For support files and downloads related to your book, please visit www.PacktPub.com.

Did you know that Packt offers eBook versions of every book published, with PDF and ePub files available? You can upgrade to the eBook version at www.PacktPub.com and as a print book customer, you are entitled to a discount on the eBook copy. Get in touch with us at service@packtpub.com for more details.

At www.PacktPub.com, you can also read a collection of free technical articles, sign up for a range of free newsletters and receive exclusive discounts and offers on Packt books and eBooks.

https://www2.packtpub.com/books/subscription/packtlib

Do you need instant solutions to your IT questions? PacktLib is Packt's online digital book library. Here, you can search, access, and read Packt's entire library of books.

Why subscribe?

- Fully searchable across every book published by Packt
- Copy and paste, print, and bookmark content
- On demand and accessible via a web browser

Free access for Packt account holders

If you have an account with Packt at www.PacktPub.com, you can use this to access PacktLib today and view 9 entirely free books. Simply use your login credentials for immediate access.

Instant updates on new Packt books

Get notified! Find out when new books are published by following @PacktEnterprise on Twitter or the *Packt Enterprise* Facebook page.

Table of Contents

Preface

Apache Camel has slowly emerged as the main framework for integration. It provides a very flexible and efficient way to integrate applications and systems all together.

Camel provides a complete set of features, based on simple but powerful concepts, allowing you to easily implement very rich integration logic.

Using this book, you will have a detailed understanding, with how to steps to implement integration logics.

What this book covers

Chapter 1, *Key Features*, introduces what Camel is and the provided key features.

Chapter 2, *Core Concepts*, introduces the basis of all the functionalities provided by Camel.

Chapter 3, *Routing and Processors*, introduces Camel routing and the usage of processors.

Chapter 4, *Beans*, explains how to use beans in Camel routes and the different registries in which the beans live.

Chapter 5, *Enterprise Integration Patterns*, introduces one of the most interesting features of Camel — the ready-to-use patterns, which serve as an answer to classic integration problems.

Chapter 6, *Components and Endpoints*, introduces Camel components and endpoints, both how to use them and implement your own.

Chapter 7, *Error Handling*, introduces how to deal with errors in Camel routes.

Chapter 8, *Testing*, introduces how to implement both unit tests and integration tests on your Camel routes.

What you need for this book

For this book, the software required will be as follows:

- Operating systems (any system supporting Java):
  - ○ Windows 7 or superior
  - ○ Unix (Linux)
- Java DK 1.7
- Apache Karaf 3.0.3

Who this book is for

This book is for developers who want to implement integration logic using Apache Camel. They will get details about Camel, from basic usage, up to the custom development of their own components.

Thanks to the first few chapters, even beginners unfamiliar with Camel will receive a comprehensive look into Camel before jumping into the details.

Conventions

In this book, you will find a number of text styles that distinguish between different kinds of information. Here are some examples of these styles and an explanation of their meaning.

Code words in text, database table names, folder names, filenames, file extensions, pathnames, dummy URLs, user input, and Twitter handles are shown as follows: " A message is described in the `org.apache.camel.Message` interface."

A block of code is set as follows:

```
public class MyProcessor implements Processor {

  public void process(Exchange exchange) {
System.out.println("Hello " +
exchange.getIn().getBody(String.class));
  }

}
```

Any command-line input or output is written as follows:

```
$ mvn clean install
```

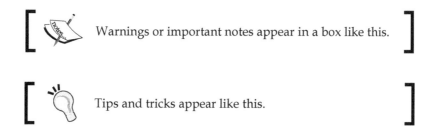

Warnings or important notes appear in a box like this.

Tips and tricks appear like this.

Reader feedback

Feedback from our readers is always welcome. Let us know what you think about this book—what you liked or disliked. Reader feedback is important for us as it helps us develop titles that you will really get the most out of.

To send us general feedback, simply e-mail feedback@packtpub.com, and mention the book's title in the subject of your message.

If there is a topic that you have expertise in and you are interested in either writing or contributing to a book, see our author guide at www.packtpub.com/authors.

Customer support

Now that you are the proud owner of a Packt book, we have a number of things to help you to get the most from your purchase.

Downloading the example code

You can download the example code files from your account at http://www.packtpub.com for all the Packt Publishing books you have purchased. If you purchased this book elsewhere, you can visit http://www.packtpub.com/support and register to have the files e-mailed directly to you.

Errata

Although we have taken every care to ensure the accuracy of our content, mistakes do happen. If you find a mistake in one of our books—maybe a mistake in the text or the code—we would be grateful if you could report this to us. By doing so, you can save other readers from frustration and help us improve subsequent versions of this book. If you find any errata, please report them by visiting `http://www.packtpub.com/submit-errata`, selecting your book, clicking on the **Errata Submission Form** link, and entering the details of your errata. Once your errata are verified, your submission will be accepted and the errata will be uploaded to our website or added to any list of existing errata under the Errata section of that title.

To view the previously submitted errata, go to `https://www.packtpub.com/books/content/support` and enter the name of the book in the search field. The required information will appear under the **Errata** section.

Piracy

Piracy of copyrighted material on the Internet is an ongoing problem across all media. At Packt, we take the protection of our copyright and licenses very seriously. If you come across any illegal copies of our works in any form on the Internet, please provide us with the location address or website name immediately so that we can pursue a remedy.

Please contact us at `copyright@packtpub.com` with a link to the suspected pirated material.

We appreciate your help in protecting our authors and our ability to bring you valuable content.

Questions

If you have a problem with any aspect of this book, you can contact us at `questions@packtpub.com`, and we will do our best to address the problem.

1
Key Features

After a quick introduction about what Apache Camel is, this chapter will introduce the key features provided by Camel. It provides just an overview of these features; the details will come in dedicated chapters.

In an enterprise, you see a lot of different software and systems in the IT ecosystem. In order to consolidate the data and sync the systems, the enterprise would want to implement communication and integration of these systems. This communication or integration is not so easy, as we have to deal with the specifications on each system the protocol and the message's data format are different most of the time, so we have to transform and adapt to each system.

Using point-to-point communication is one option. However, the problem with this approach is that we tighten the integration of a couple of systems. Changing to other systems or protocols requires refactoring of the implementation. Moreover, dealing with multiple systems is not so easy with point-to-point.

So, instead of point-to-point, we use mediation. Mediation reduces complexity and provides a more flexible approach by adding and using a tier between the systems (man in the middle). The purpose is to facilitate the information flow and integration of the systems.

Apache Camel is a mediation framework.

What is Apache Camel?

Apache Camel originated in Apache ServiceMix. Apache ServiceMix 3 was powered by the Spring framework and implemented in the JBI specification. The **Java Business Integration (JBI)** specification proposed a Plug and Play approach for integration problems. JBI was based on WebService concepts and standards. For instance, it directly reuses the **Message Exchange Patterns (MEP)** concept that comes from **WebService Description Language (WSDL)**.

Camel reuses some of these concepts, for instance, you will see that we have the concept of MEP in Camel.

However, JBI suffered mostly from two issues:

- In JBI, all messages between endpoints are transported in the **Normalized Messages Router** (**NMR**).

  In the NMR, a message has a standard XML format. As all messages in the NMR have the same format, it's easy to audit messages and the format is predictable.

  However, the JBI XML format has an important drawback for performances: it needs to marshall and unmarshall the messages. Some protocols (such as REST or RMI) are not easy to describe in XML.

  For instance, REST can work in stream mode. It doesn't make sense to marshall streams in XML.

  Camel is payload-agnostic. This means that you can transport any kind of messages with Camel (not necessary XML formatted).

- JBI describes a packaging. We distinguish the binding components (responsible for the interaction with the system outside of the NMR and the handling of the messages in the NMR), and the service engines (responsible for transforming the messages inside the NMR).

  However, it's not possible to directly deploy the endpoints based on these components. JBI requires a service unit (a ZIP file) per endpoint, and for each package in a service assembly (another ZIP file). JBI also splits the description of the endpoint from its configuration.

  It does not result in a very flexible packaging: with definitions and configurations scattered in different files, not easy to maintain. In Camel, the configuration and definition of the endpoints are gathered in a simple URI. It's easier to read.

  Moreover, Camel doesn't force any packaging; the same definition can be packaged in a simple XML file, OSGi bundle, and regular JAR file.

In addition to JBI, another foundation of Camel is the book *Enterprise Integration Patterns by Gregor Hohpe and Bobby Woolf*.

This book describes design patterns answering classical problems while dealing with enterprise application integration and message oriented middleware.

The book describes the problems and the patterns to solve them. Camel strives to implement the patterns described in the book to make them easy to use and let the developer concentrate on the task at hand.

This is what Camel is: an open source framework that allows you to integrate systems and that comes with a lot of connectors and **Enterprise Integration Patterns (EIP)** components out of the box. And if that is not enough, one can extend and implement custom components.

Components and bean support

Apache Camel ships with a wide variety of components out of the box; currently, there are more than 100 components available.

We can see:

- The connectivity components that allow exposure of endpoints for external systems or communicate with external systems. For instance, the FTP, HTTP, JMX, WebServices, JMS, and a lot more components are connectivity components. Creating an endpoint and the associated configuration for these components is easy, by directly using a URI.
- The internal components applying rules to the messages internally to Camel. These kinds of components apply validation or transformation rules to the inflight message. For instance, validation or XSLT are internal components.

Thanks to this, Camel brings a very powerful connectivity and mediation framework.

Moreover, it's pretty easy to create new custom components, allowing you to extend Camel if the default components set doesn't match your requirements.

It's also very easy to implement complex integration logic by creating your own processors and reusing your beans. Camel supports beans frameworks (IoC), such as Spring or Blueprint.

Predicates and expressions

As we will see later, most of the EIP need a rule definition to apply a routing logic to a message. The rule is described using an expression.

It means that we have to define expressions or predicates in the Enterprise Integration Patterns. An expression returns any kind of value, whereas a predicate returns true or false only.

Camel supports a lot of different languages to declare expressions or predicates. It doesn't force you to use one, it allows you to use the most appropriate one.

For instance, Camel supports xpath, mvel, ognl, python, ruby, PHP, JavaScript, SpEL (Spring Expression Language), Groovy, and so on as expression languages. It also provides native Camel prebuilt functions and languages that are easy to use such as header, constant, or simple languages.

Data format and type conversion

Camel is payload-agnostic. This means that it can support any kind of message. Depending on the endpoints, it could be required to convert from one format to another. That's why Camel supports different data formats, in a pluggable way. This means that Camel can marshall or unmarshall a message in a given format. For instance, in addition to the standard JVM serialization, Camel natively supports Avro, JSON, protobuf, JAXB, XmlBeans, XStream, JiBX, SOAP, and so on.

Depending on the endpoints and your need, you can explicitly define the data format during the processing of the message. On the other hand, Camel knows the expected format and type of endpoints. Thanks to this, Camel looks for a type converter, allowing to implicitly transform a message from one format to another.

You can also explicitly define the type converter of your choice at some points during the processing of the message. Camel provides a set of ready-to-use type converters, but, as Camel supports a pluggable model, you can extend it by providing your own type converters. It's a simple POJO to implement.

Easy configuration and URI

Camel uses a different approach based on URI. The endpoint itself and its configuration are on the URI.

The URI is human readable and provides the details of the endpoint, which is the endpoint component and the endpoint configuration.

As this URI is part of the complete configuration (which defines what we name a route, as we will see later), it's possible to have a complete overview of the integration logic and connectivity in a row. We will cover this in detail in *Chapter 2, Core Concepts*.

Lightweight and different deployment topologies

Camel itself is very light. The Camel core is only around 2 MB, and contains everything required to run Camel. As it's based on a pluggable architecture, all Camel components are provided as external modules, allowing you to install only what you need, without installing superfluous and needlessly heavy modules.

As we saw, Camel is based on simple POJO, which means that the Camel core doesn't depend on other frameworks: it's an atomic framework and is ready to use. All other modules (components, DSL, and so on) are built on top of this Camel core.

Moreover, Camel is not tied to one container for deployment. Camel supports a wide range of containers to run. They are as follows:

- A J2EE application server such as WebSphere, WebLogic, JBoss, and so on
- A Web container such as Apache Tomcat
- An OSGi container such as Apache Karaf
- A standalone application using frameworks such as Spring

Camel gives a lot of flexibility, allowing you to embed it into your application or to use an enterprise-ready container.

Quick prototyping and testing support

In any integration project, it's typical that we have some part of the integration logic not yet available. For instance:

- The application to integrate with has not yet been purchased or not yet ready
- The remote system to integrate with has a heavy cost, not acceptable during the development phase
- Multiple teams work in parallel, so we may have some kinds of deadlocks between the teams

As a complete integration framework, Camel provides a very easy way to prototype part of the integration logic. Even if you don't have the actual system to integrate, you can simulate this system (mock), as it allows you to implement your integration logic without waiting for dependencies. The mocking support is directly part of the Camel core and doesn't require any additional dependency.

Along the same lines, testing is also crucial in an integration project. In such a kind of project, a lot of errors can happen and most are unforeseen. Moreover, a small change in an integration process might impact a lot of other processes. Camel provides the tools to easily test your design and integration logic, allowing you to integrate this in a continuous integration platform.

Management and monitoring using JMX

Apache Camel uses the Java Management Extension (JMX) standard and provides a lot of insights into the system using MBeans (Management Beans), providing a detailed view of the following current system:

- The different integration processes with the associated metrics
- The different components and endpoints with the associated metrics

Moreover, these MBeans provide more insights than metrics. They also provide the operations to manage Camel. For instance, the operations allow you to stop an integration process, to suspend an endpoint, and so on. Using a combination of metrics and operations, you can configure a very agile integration solution.

Active community

The Apache Camel community is very active. This means that potential issues are identified very quickly and a fix is available soon after. However, it also means that a lot of ideas and contributions are proposed, giving more and more features to Camel.

Another big advantage of an active community is that you will never be alone; a lot of people are active on the mailing lists who are ready to answer your question and provide advice.

Apache Camel is an enterprise integration solution used in many large organizations with enterprise support available through RedHat or Talend.

Summary

This chapter briefly introduced Camel and where it's come from. It mainly introduced Camel's key features. In the next chapter, before dealing with some of these features in detail, we will introduce the Camel core concepts, which will help you easily understand the further chapters.

2
Core Concepts

This chapter introduces the core concepts of Camel. These concepts are the key basis of all functionalities provided by Camel. We will use them in the next chapters. As we have seen in the previous chapter, Camel is an integration framework. This means that it provides everything to implement your mediation logic: messaging, routing, transformation, and connectivity.

We will look at the following concepts:

- Messages
- Exchanges
- Camel contexts

Messages

Messages transport the data between the different parts of the mediation logic. Your mediation logic will define the flow of messages between different nodes.

A message flows in one direction, from a sender to a receiver. It's not possible to use the same message to answer the sender, we will have to use another message. A message is described in the `org.apache.camel.Message` interface.

The javadoc is available at `http://camel.apache.org/maven/camel-2.13.0/camel-core/apidocs/org/apache/camel/Message.html`.

A message contains the following:

- ID: A message ID of type `String`. Camel creates an ID for you. This ID identifies the message and can be used for correlation or storage. For instance, we will see that the message ID is used in the idempotent consumer pattern to identify the message in a store.

- Header: A set of headers, allowing you to store any kind of data associated with a message. The headers are stored as `org.apache.camel.util.CaseInsensitiveMap` by default. The `CaseInsensitiveMap` (`http://camel.apache.org/maven/camel-2.13.0/camel-core/apidocs/org/apache/camel/util/CaseInsensitiveMap.html`) extends `HashMap<String,Object>`. This means you can store any kinds of objects (including very large objects) in the header. To access the map use a `String` key, which is case insensitive. The lifetime of the headers is the same as the message (as the headers are part of the message itself). The purpose of the headers is to add hints about the content encoding, authentication information, and so on. As we will see in the next chapters, Camel itself uses and populates the headers for its own needs and configurations.

- Attachment: A set of attachments is mostly to match the requirements of some protocols and components: WebService component (to provide SOAP Message Transmission Optimization Mechanism (MTOM) support) or the e-mail component (to provide support for e-mail attachments). The attachments are only used by some dedicated components, they are not as heavily used as the headers. The attachments are stored in the message as `Map<String,DataHandler>`. An attachment name is a `String`, which is case sensitive. An attachment is stored using `DataHandler` providing support of MIME type and consistent access to the data.

- Fault flag: A fault flag Boolean that allows you to distinguish whether the message is a normal message or a faulted message. It allows some components or patterns to treat the message in a different way. For instance, instead of a SOAP Response, a message may contain a SOAP Fault. In that case, we have to inform the component that a message containing a SOAP Fault is not a normal message.

- Body: The body is the actual payload of the message. The body is stored as an `Object` in the message, allowing you to store any kind of data. In *Chapter 1, Key Features* we saw that one of the Camel key features is to be payload-agnostic. The fact that the body is directly an `Object` is the implementation of the payload-agnostic feature.

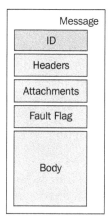

Exchange

Camel doesn't transport a message directly. The main reason is that a message flows only in one direction. When dealing with messaging, there are many Message Exchange Patterns (MEP) that we can use.

Depending on the use cases, we can send a message without expecting any return from the destination: this pattern is named event message and uses InOnlyMEP. For instance, when you read a file from the filesystem, you just process the file content, without returning anything to the endpoint that read the file. In that case, the component responsible for reading the filesystem will define an InOnlyMEP.

On the other hand, you may want to implement a request reply pattern: a response message should be returned to the sender of the request message, and so it uses an InOutMEP. For instance, you receive a SOAP Request from a WebService component, so you should return a SOAP Response (or SOAP Fault) to the message sender.

In Camel, MEP are described in the `org.apache.camel.ExchangePattern` enumeration (`http://camel.apache.org/maven/current/camel-core/apidocs/org/apache/camel/ExchangePattern.html`). We can see that Camel supports the following MEP:

- InOnly
- InOptionalOut
- InOut
- OutIn
- OutOptionalIn

- RobustInOnly
- RobustOutOnly

As a message flows in only one direction, in order to support the different MEPs, we need two messages:

- The first message is mandatory as it's the `in` message
- The second message is optional (depending on the MEP) as it's the `out` message

That's why Camel **wraps** the messages into an Exchange object: the actual object transported is the Exchange, acting as a messages container with all meta-data required for the routing logic.

This Exchange object is used for the complete mediation process execution.

The `org.apache.camel.Exchange` interface describes an exchange.

Basically, an exchange contains the following:

- Exchange ID: An exchange ID as a `String`. This is a unique identifier for the exchange. Camel creates it for you.
- MEP: The Message Exchange Pattern (MEP) defines the exchange pattern.
- Exception: The `Exception` is used by the error handler, as we will see later. It stores the current cause of an exchange failure. If an error occurs at any time during routing, it will be set in this exception field.
- Properties: The properties is a `Map<String, Object>` and may look like message headers. The main difference is their lifetime: the properties exist during the whole exchange execution, whereas the headers are limited to the message duration (and a message can change a lot during routing, so during the exchange execution). Camel itself may add some properties for some use cases.
- Finally, we have the `in` and `out` messages.
    - In Message: The `in` message is mandatory and always set. It's the only message populated in the exchange with InOnlyMEP.
    - Out Message: The `out` message is optional and is only used with InOutMEP.

With InOutMEP, at the end of the processing of the exchange, the out message will be used and returned to the mediation beginner (the first endpoint of the routing who created the exchange).

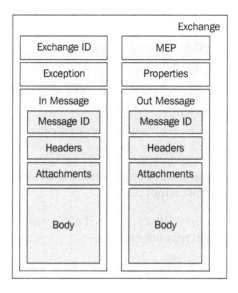

Camel context

The Camel context is the runtime system and the loading container of all resources required for the execution of the routing. It keeps everything together to allow the user to execute the routing logic. When the context starts, it also starts various components and endpoints, and activates the routing rules.

The Camel context is described by the org.apache.camel.CamelContext interface (http://camel.apache.org/maven/current/camel-core/apidocs/org/apache/camel/CamelContext.html).

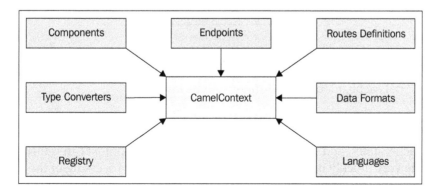

A Camel context contains the following:

- The components and endpoints used in the routing (see later for the details about components and endpoints)
- The type converters used to transform a message of one type to another
- The data formats used to define the format of a message body
- The registry where Camel will look for the beans used in the routing
- The languages describing expressions and predicates used in the routing by a language (xpath, xquery, PHP, and so on)
- The routes definition itself allowing you to design your mediation logic

Most of these resources are automatically loaded by Camel for you; most of the time, as an end user, you specify the routes definitions. However, we will see in the next chapters that we can tweak the Camel context.

A Camel context also has its own life cycle. As it's the runtime system of your routing, you have a control on this life cycle.

A Camel context can be started, loading all resources needed and activating the routing logic.

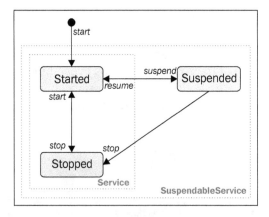

Once started, a context can be stopped: it's a cold stop. This means that all routes, components, endpoints, and other resources loaded by this context will be stopped, and all internal cache, metrics, and states will be lost.

Instead of stopped, from the started state, a context can be suspended. Suspend stops the routing of the messages, but keeps context resources loaded and the internal data (metrics, cache, states, and so on). That's why a suspended context can return to the started state very quickly using resume: it just resumes the processing of the messages.

The end users are supposed to use only suspend and resume operations.

To restart a context, you can do the following:

- A hot restart using suspend operation first, and resume operation after. It's a fast restart, keeping all the internal data of the context.
- A cold restart using the stop operation first, and the start operation later. In that case, all internal data (cache, states, and metrics) is lost.

Both stop and resume operations will ensure that all inflight messages (messages currently in process) are completely processed.

Stopping or suspending a context will stop or suspend all the routing defined in this context. In order to guarantee a graceful and reliable shutdown of your routing, you can define a shutdown strategy.

A shutdown strategy is described using the `org.apache.camel.spi.ShutdownStrategy` interface.

Camel provides the `org.apache.camel.impl.DefaultShutdownStrategy` interface.

This default shutdown strategy works in two phases:

1. First, it does a graceful shutdown, by suspending or stopping all consumer (the first endpoint that creates the exchanges), and waiting for the completion of all inflight messages.
2. After a timeout (5 minutes by default), if there are still some inflight messages, the strategy kills the exchanges, forcing a suspend or stop.

We will see in the next chapters how to create and use our own shutdown strategy.

Processor

A processor is a node in the routing which is able to use, create, or modify an incoming exchange. During routing, the exchanges flow from one processor to another. This means all Enterprise Integration Patterns (EIP) are implemented using processors in Camel. The exchanges get in and out of a processor by using components and endpoints, as we will see later in this chapter.

A processor is described using the `org.apache.camel.Processor` interface. To create your own processor, you just have to implement the `Processor` interface and override the `process()` method:

```
public class MyProcessor implements Processor {

  public void process(Exchange exchange) {
System.out.println("Hello " +
exchange.getIn().getBody(String.class));
  }

}
```

Thanks to the `Exchange` argument of the `process()` method, you have complete access to the exchange: in and out messages, properties, and so on.

The `exchange.getIn()` gets the `in` message of the current exchange. As we want to get the body of this message, we use the `getBody()` method. This method accepts a type argument, casting the body in the destination class (a string in our example).

Routes

The Camel route is the routing definition. It's a graph of processors. The routes (routing definition) are loaded in the Camel context. The execution and flow of the exchange in a route is performed by the routing engine. The routes are used to decouple clients from servers, and producers from consumers: an exchange consumer doesn't know where the exchange comes from, and on the other hand an exchange producer doesn't know the destination of the exchange. Thanks to that, it provides a flexible way to add extra processing or change the routing with limited impact on the logic.

Each route has a unique identifier that you can specify (or Camel will create one for you). This identifier is used to easily find the route, especially when you want to log, debug, monitor, or manage a route (start or stop).

A route has exactly one input source (the input endpoint). A route has a life cycle similar to the Camel context with the same states: started, stopped, and suspended. To Camel, a context controls the life cycle of the routes that it contains.

Channels

In every Camel route, there is a channel that sits between each processor in the route graph. It's responsible for the routing of an Exchange to the next Processor in the graph. The channel acts as a controller that monitors and controls the routing at runtime. It allows Camel to enrich the route with interceptors. For instance, the Camel tracer or the error handling are functionalities implemented using an interceptor on the channel.

The channel is described by the `org.apache.camel.Channel` interface. You can configure your own interceptor on the channels by describing it in Camel context.

Camel supports three kinds of interceptors on the channels:

- Global interceptors: This intercepts all exchanges on the channels
- Interceptors on the incoming exchanges: This has limited the scope of the interceptor only on the first channel (the one just after the first endpoint)
- Interceptors on the exchanges going to one specific endpoint: This limits the interceptor to the channel just before a given endpoint

Domain Specific Languages (DSL)

Using the Camel API directly would need you to write a lot of plumbing code. You will need to create all the objects and load a lot of objects into different ones.

Therefore, the direct usage of API would be very time consuming. Moreover, as a flexible and easy-to-use integration framework, Camel doesn't have to force the use of one language (Java) to write the routing logic. Users may not be familiar with Java and might prefer to write their routing logic using another language.

That's why Camel provides a set of languages to directly write the routes: the Camel Domain Specific Languages (DSL).

Using a DSL, the user directly writes their routes and describes the Camel context using a DSL. Camel will load and interpret the DSL to create and instantiate all the objects.

The DSL is used to wire processors and endpoints together to define and form routes.

Using a DSL, you mostly define the following:

- The Camel context containing the routing rule base and resources
- The routes definition

Camel supports the following DSL:

- Java DSL, allowing you to define the routes using a fluent Java API
- Spring XML, allowing you to define the routes using XML and the Spring framework
- Blueprint XML is similar to Spring XML but uses OSGi Blueprint instead of the Spring framework
- REST DSL, allowing you to define the routes using a REST style API (in Java or XML)
- Groovy DSL, allowing you to define the routes using the Groovy language
- Scala DSL, allowing you to define the routes using the Scala language
- Annotation DSL, allowing you to define the routes directly using annotations on Beans

The following routes are exactly the same, but written using two different DSLs.

Using Java DSL:

```
from("file:/inbox").to("jms:queue:orders")
```

Using Spring or Blueprint DSL:

```
<route>
<from uri="file:/inbox"/>
<to uri="jms:queue:orders"/>
</route>
```

Component, endpoint, producer, and consumer

The components are the main extension points in Camel. We don't directly use a component in a route, we define an endpoint from the component. This means a component acts as a factory for endpoints as follows:

- First, you load the component in the Camel context
- Then, in the route definition, you define an endpoint on a component loaded in the Camel context

You can explicitly instantiate a component and load it in the Camel context (using code), or Camel will try to create and load the component (discover) for you based on the endpoint definition.

Camel provides about 100 components (file, ftp, http, CXF, JMS, and so on) as you can see at `http://camel.apache.org/components.html`. You can create your own component, as we will see in the next chapters.

Using a component, we create the endpoints. An endpoint represents the end of a channel through which an external system can send or receive messages. It allows your Camel route to communicate with the environment.

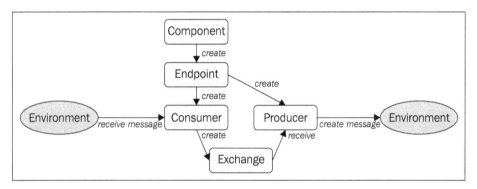

Depending on the location in the route, an endpoint can act as follows:

- A producer receives a Camel Exchange, transforms it into an external message and communicates (sends the message) to the external system (environment)
- A consumer receives a message from an external system (environment), wraps it as a Camel Exchange, and sends to the route

We identify two kinds of consumers:

- Event Driven Consumers who will listen for incoming messages and create a Camel exchange at this time. For instance, consumer endpoints using the CXF component will **react** when they receive a SOAP Request.
- Polling Consumers who periodically check for new resources and create a Camel exchange at this time. For instance, consumer endpoints using the File component will periodically poll the filesystem and create a Camel exchange for the new files.

The endpoints are described using a URI in the following format:

```
component:option?option=value&option=value
```

For instance, we can define an endpoint of the file component using the following code:

```
file:data/inbox?delay=5000&noop=true
```

At runtime, Camel will look up an endpoint based on the URI, check whether the component defined as prefix is in the Camel context (eventually load it, if it's not there), and use this component to actually create the endpoint.

Data format

Camel supports a pluggable data format allowing you to marshall and unmarshall the messages.

For instance, if you receive an XML message from an endpoint, you can:

- Directly manipulate and transport the XML message in the route
- Translate the XML to a POJO using JAXB, for instance, JAXB is a data format

Unmarshalling allows you to use a data format to convert from a raw format (XML in the previous example) into a Java object. On the other hand, when you send an exchange to an endpoint, you can marshall the transported object into another format. You specify where you want to unmarshall or marshall and the data format to use.

For instance, you can consume an XML message from a JMS queue, unmarshall using JAXB, and send the resulting object to another JMS queue:

```
from("jms:queue:orders").unmarshal("jaxb").to("jms:queue:other")
```

You can also unmarshall files containing a serialized object, and then marshall using JAXB to send the resulting XML message to a JMS queue:

```
from("file:data/inbox").unmarshal().serialization().marshall("jaxb").
to("jms:queue:orders")
```

Camel provides a lot of ready-to-use data formats:

- For JVM native serialization marshalling, you can use the serialization or Stringdata formats
- For object marshalling, you can use Avro, JSON, or Protobuf data formats

- For XML data formats (marshalling and unmarshalling), you can use JAXB, XmlBeans, XStream, JiBX, or Castor libraries

- For XML or WebService marshalling, you can use the SOAP data format

- For XML or JSON marshalling, you can use the XmlJson data format

- For flat data structure marshalling (CSV, DelimitedLength, and so on), you can use BeanIO, Bindy, CSV, EDI, or Flatpack data formats

- For compression marshalling, you can use GZip or Zip data formats

- For security marshalling, you can use PGP, Crypto, or XML Sec data formats

- For other marshalling, you can use Base64, RSS, TidyMarkup (with HTML, for instance), or Syslog data formats

You can also create your own data format, providing the custom marshalling and unmarshalling mechanism.

Type converter

Even without a data format, when you route a message from one endpoint to another, it's common to convert the body of the message from one type to another. For instance, in an exchange created by a file endpoint, the body of the in message will be an InputStream. Depending on the target endpoint or processor, we may want to convert this InputStream to a String.

When you use the `getBody()` method on a message, you can specify the expected type. Camel will use a type converter to try to convert the actual body of the message into the specified type.

For instance, in a processor, if you do the following:

```
Message in = exchange.getIn();
Document document = in.getBody(Document.class);
```

Camel will try to convert the body of the in message into a DOM document. A type converter is defined by the `org.apache.camel.TypeConverter` interface. The type converters are loaded into the Camel context, in a type converter's registry.

The type converter's registry contains the type converter with the supported types. In this registry, for each type converter, we have:

- The **source** type
- The **destination** type
- The actual type converter instance

For instance, we can add our own type converter in the Camel context as follows:

```
context.getTypeConverterRegistry().addTypeConverter(MyOrder.class,
String.class, new MyOrderTypeConverter());
```

We can see that the source type is `MyOrder`, the destination type is `String`, and to convert from a type `MyOrder` to `String`, I will use the `MyOrderTypeConverter()` method.

Summary

We can see that even if the Camel core is light, the provided features are rich and it provides all the basics to extend Camel to match your needs.

This chapter is an introduction to the Camel core concepts. It allows you to easily understand the next chapters, where we will get into the details of Camel.

3
Routing and Processors

In the previous chapter, we saw the core concepts of implementing the messaging and routing system provided by Camel.

In this chapter we will cover routing — one of the most important features of Camel. Without the routing, Camel would be a simple *connectivity* framework. Routing is a key function of Camel, it means we can apply all the transformations to a message. It can modify the content of the message itself or the destination of the message, all on the fly.

This chapter introduces:

- How to use a processor to change an exchange
- A complete example of a route containing a processor

What is a processor?

A consumer endpoint receives an event from the environment and wraps it as an **Exchange**.

The routing engine transports this Exchange from the endpoint to a processor, which is possible from one processor to another processor, up to a final endpoint via a **Channel**. The route can end at a processor returning the Exchange to the consumer endpoint if the MEP is InOut (and using the out message), or stop with a producer endpoint, sending the message to the environment.

This means that a processor acts as an Exchange modifier — it consumes an Exchange, and eventually updates it. We can see the processor as a message translator. Actually, all Camel **Exchange Integration Patterns** (**EIPs**) are implemented using processors.

A processor is described by the org.apache.camel.Processor interface. This interface provides only one method:

```
void process(Exchange exchange) throws Exception(Exchange
exchange) throws Exception
```

As the processor directly receives an Exchange, it has access to all the data contained in the Exchange:

1. The message exchange pattern
2. The in message
3. The out message
4. The exchange exception

An example of Camel routes containing processors

Here we will illustrate the use of processors in an example. This example will create an **OSGi** bundle, which will create two Camel contexts with one route in each; they are as follows:

- One route using the Camel Java DSL
- One route using the Camel Blueprint DSL

First, we create the Maven project pom.xml for our bundle:

```xml
<?xml version="1.0" encoding="UTF-8"?>
<project xmlns="http://maven.apache.org/POM/4.0.0"
xmlns:xsi="http://www.w3.org/2001/XMLSchema-instance"
xsi:schemaLocation="http://maven.apache.org/POM/4.0.0
http://maven.apache.org/xsd/maven-4.0.0.xsd">

    <modelVersion>4.0.0</modelVersion>

    <groupId>com.packt.camel</groupId>
    <artifactId>chapter3</artifactId>
    <version>1.0-SNAPSHOT</version>
    <packaging>bundle</packaging>

    <dependencies>
        <dependency>
            <groupId>org.apache.camel</groupId>
            <artifactId>camel-core</artifactId>
```

```
                <version>2.12.4</version>
            </dependency>
            <dependency>
                <groupId>org.osgi</groupId>
                <artifactId>org.osgi.core</artifactId>
                <version>4.3.1</version>
                <scope>provided</scope>
            </dependency>
        </dependencies>

        <build>
            <plugins>
                <plugin>
                    <groupId>org.apache.felix</groupId>
                    <artifactId>maven-bundle-plugin</artifactId>
                    <version>2.3.7</version>
                    <extensions>true</extensions>
                    <configuration>
                        <instructions>
                            <Import-Package>*</Import-Package>
                            <Bundle-Activator>
                              com.packt.camel.chapter3.Activator
                                </Bundle-Activator>
                        </instructions>
                    </configuration>
                </plugin>
            </plugins>
        </build>

    </project>
```

In this `pom.xml`, we can see:

- That we depend on camel-core (in the version of our choice; here it's 2.12.3)
- We also depend to osgi-core as we create an OSGi bundle
- We use the maven-bundle plugin to create the OSGi bundle (especially the MANIFEST containing the OSGi headers). Here, we provide a bundle Activator (`com.pack.camel.chapter3.Activator`), the details of which we will see later in this chapter.

Prefixer processor

We are now ready to create a Prefixer processor. This processor will get the incoming Exchange, extract the `in` message body, and prefix this body with *Prefixed*.

The processor is a simple class implementing the Camel processor interface.

We create `PrefixerProcessor` as follows:

```
package com.packt.camel.chapter3;

import org.apache.camel.Exchange;
import org.apache.camel.Processor;
import org.slf4j.Logger;
import org.slf4j.LoggerFactory;

public class PrefixerProcessor implements Processor {

  private final static Logger LOGGER = LoggerFactory.
getLogger(PrefixerProcessor.class);

  public void process(Exchange exchange) throws Exception {
      String inBody = exchange.getIn().getBody(String.class);
      LOGGER.info("Received in message with body {}", inBody);
      LOGGER.info("Prefixing body ...");
      inBody = "Prefixed " + inBody;
      exchange.getIn().setBody(inBody);
  }

}
```

Here, we can see how the processor acts as a message translator; it transforms the `in` message.

Creating a route using Java DSL

It's now time to create the first route using the Camel Java DSL, using the `PrefixerProcessor`. In order to use the Camel Java DSL, we create a class extending the Camel `RouteBuilder` class (`org.apache.camel.RouteBuilder`). This class describes the route in a `configure()` method.

We create a `MyRouteBuilder` class which is as follows:

```
package com.packt.camel.chapter3;

import org.apache.camel.Exchange;
```

```
import org.apache.camel.Processor;
import org.apache.camel.builder.RouteBuilder;

public class MyRouteBuilder extends RouteBuilder {

  public void configure() {
      from("timer:fire?period=5000")
              .setBody(constant("Hello Chapter3"))
              .process(new PrefixerProcessor())
              .to("log:MyRoute")
              .process(new Processor() {
                  public void process(Exchange exchange)
                    throws Exception {
                    String body =
                       exchange.getIn().getBody(String.class);
                    if (body.startsWith("Prefixed ")) {
                        body = body.substring
                           ("Prefixed ".length());
                        exchange.getIn().setBody(body);
                    }
                  }
              })
              .to("log:MyRoute");
    }

}
```

This route starts with a timer. The timer creates an empty Exchange every 5 seconds.

We define the body of the `in` message (of this Exchange) using the `.setBody()` method, containing the `Hello Chapter3` constant String.

We call `PrefixerProcessor` using the `.process()` method. As expected, the `PrefixerProcessor` appends `Prefixed` to the body of the `in` message, resulting to `Prefixed Hello Chapter3`. We can see that `PrefixerProcesser` has been correctly called using a log endpoint just after (`.to("log:MyRoute")`).

Instead of creating a dedicated class for a processor, it's also possible to create a processor inline. It's what we do using `.process(new Processor() {...})`. We implement an inline processor that removes the prefix appended by `PrefixerProcessor`.

Finally, we can see that we are back to the original message in the latest log endpoint (`.to("log:MyRoute")`).

The `MyRouteBuilder` class is the route builder. A route has to be embedded in the `CamelContext`. It's the purpose of our bundle Activator; the Activator creates the `CamelContext`, builds the route, and registers the route in this `CamelContext`. For convenience, we also register the `CamelContext` as an OSGi service (it allows us to see the `CamelContext` and the route using the `camel:*` Karaf commands).

The `Activator` is a class implementing the `BundleActivator` interface (`org.osgi.framework.BundleActivator`):

```
package com.packt.camel.chapter3;

import org.apache.camel.CamelContext;
import org.apache.camel.impl.DefaultCamelContext;
import org.osgi.framework.BundleActivator;
import org.osgi.framework.BundleContext;
import org.osgi.framework.ServiceRegistration;

public class Activator implements BundleActivator {

  private CamelContext camelContext;
  private ServiceRegistration serviceRegistration;

  public void start(BundleContext bundleContext) throws Exception {
      camelContext = new DefaultCamelContext();
      camelContext.addRoutes(new MyRouteBuilder());
      serviceRegistration = bundleContext.registerService
        (CamelContext.class, camelContext, null);
      camelContext.start();
  }

  public void stop(BundleContext bundleContext) throws Exception {
      if (serviceRegistration != null) {
        serviceRegistration.unregister();
      }
      if (camelContext != null) {
        camelContext.stop();
      }
  }

}
```

When the bundle starts, the `start()` method of the `Activator` is called by the OSGi framework.

At startup, we create the `CamelContext` using `new DefaultCamelContext()`.

We create and register our route in this `CamelContext` using `camelContext. addRoutes(new MyRouteBuilder())`.

For convenience, we register the `CamelContext` as an OSGi service using `bundleContext.registerService(CamelContext.class, camelContext, null)`. Thanks to this service registration, our `CamelContext` and route will be visible for the Camel:* commands that we have in the Apache Karaf OSGi container.

Finally, we start the Camel Context (and the route) using `camelContext.start()`.

On the other hand, when we stop the bundle, the OSGi framework will call the `stop()` method of the Activator.

In the `stop()` method, we unregister the Camel Context OSGi service (using `serviceRegistration.unregister()`) and we stop the Camel Context (using `camelContext.stop()`).

Route using Camel Blueprint DSL

In the same bundle, we can create another Camel Context and design another route, but this time using the Camel Blueprint DSL (OSGi specific). When using the Camel Blueprint DSL, we don't have to write all the plumbing code as we do for the first Camel Context. The Camel Context is implicitly created by Camel, and we declare the route in the Camel Context using the XML description.

In the `OSGI-INF/blueprint` folder of our bundle, we create `route.xml`:

```xml
<?xml version="1.0" encoding="UTF-8"?>
<blueprint xmlns="http://www.osgi.org/xmlns/blueprint/v1.0.0">

  <bean id="prefixerProcessor" class="com.packt.camel.chapter3.
PrefixerProcessor"/>

  <camelContext xmlns="http://camel.apache.org/schema/blueprint">
      <route>
          <from uri="timer:fire?period=5000"/>
          <setBody>
              <constant>Hello Chapter3</constant>
          </setBody>
          <process ref="prefixerProcessor"/>
          <to uri="log:blueprintRoute"/>
      </route>
  </camelContext>

</blueprint>
```

In this Blueprint descriptor, we first create the `prefixerProcessor` bean. The Blueprint container will create the processor.

The Camel Blueprint DSL provides the `<camelContext/>` element. Camel will create the Camel Context for us and register the route that we describe. The `<route/>` element allows us to describe the route.

Basically, the route is very close to the previous one:

- It starts with a timer, creating an empty Exchange every 5 seconds.
- It sets the body to `Hello Chapter3`.
- It calls the `prefixerProcessor`. In this case, we use the reference to the registered bean. The `ref="prefixerProcessor"` corresponds to the `id="prefixerProcessor"` of the `PrefixerProcessor` bean.
- We also call a log endpoint.

It's important to understand that even if we use the same class, we have two different instances of `PrefixerProcessor`:

- A first instance is created in the bundle `Activator` and used in the route described using the Camel Java DSL
- A second instance is created in the `blueprint` container and used in the route described using the Camel Blueprint DSL

Building and deploying our bundle, we are now ready to build our bundle.

Using Maven, we just run the following command:

```
$ mvn clean install

...
[INFO] ------------------------------------------------------------------
------
[INFO] BUILD SUCCESS
[INFO] ------------------------------------------------------------------
------
[INFO] Total time: 4.489s
[INFO] Finished at: Thu Sep 11 15:14:42 CEST 2014
[INFO] Final Memory: 33M/1188M
[INFO] ------------------------------------------------------------------
------
```

Our bundle is now available in our local Maven repository (by default, in the `.m2/repository` folder of the `home` directory).

We are ready to deploy the bundle in the Karaf OSGi container.

After having started Karaf (using `bin/karaf` for instance, providing the Karaf shell console), we first have to install the Camel support. For this, we register the camel features repository and install the `camel-blueprint` feature.

The `camel-blueprint` feature provides support for Camel core (so the Camel Java DSL, and all core classes such as `CamelContext`, `Processor`, and so on), and Camel Blueprint DSL.

To register the Camel features repository, we use the Karaf `feature:repo-add` command specifying the Camel version we want to use:

```
karaf@root()> feature:repo-add camel 2.12.3

Adding feature url mvn:org.apache.camel.karaf/apache-
camel/2.12.3/xml/features
```

We install the `camel-blueprint` feature using the `feature:install` command:

```
karaf@root()> feature:install -v camel-blueprint

Installing feature camel-blueprint 2.12.3

Installing feature camel-core 2.12.3

Installing feature xml-specs-api 2.2.0

Found installed bundle: org.apache.servicemix.specs.activation-api-
1.1 [78]

Found installed bundle: org.apache.servicemix.specs.stax-api-1.0 [79]

Found installed bundle: org.apache.servicemix.specs.jaxb-api-2.2 [80]

Found installed bundle: stax2-api [81]

Found installed bundle: woodstox-core-asl [82]

Found installed bundle: org.apache.servicemix.bundles.jaxb-impl [83]

Found installed bundle: org.apache.camel.camel-core [84]

Found installed bundle: org.apache.camel.karaf.camel-karaf-commands
[85]

Found installed bundle: org.apache.camel.camel-blueprint [86]
```

We are now ready to install and start our bundle.

For the installation, we use the `bundle:install` command with the Maven location defined in the `pom.xml`:

```
karaf@root()> bundle:install mvn:com.packt.camel/chapter3/1.0-
SNAPSHOT

Bundle ID: 87
```

We start the bundle using the `bundle:start` command using the `Bundle ID` given by the previous command:

```
karaf@root()> bundle:start 87
```

The log messages shows that our routes are running (using the `log:display` command):

```
karaf@root()> log:display
...
2014-09-11 15:25:45,542 | INFO  | 0 - timer://fire | MyRoute
  | 84 - org.apache.camel.camel-core - 2.12.3 | Exchange[ExchangePattern:
InOnly, BodyType: String, Body: Prefixed Hello Chapter3]
2014-09-11 15:25:45,543 | INFO  | 0 - timer://fire | MyRoute
  | 84 - org.apache.camel.camel-core - 2.12.3 | Exchange[ExchangePattern:
InOnly, BodyType: String, Body: Hello Chapter3]
2014-09-11 15:25:46,253 | INFO  | 2 - timer://fire | PrefixerProcessor
| 87 - com.packt.camel.chapter3 - 1.0.0.SNAPSHOT | Received in message
with body Hello Chapter3
2014-09-11 15:25:46,253 | INFO  | 2 - timer://fire | PrefixerProcessor
| 87 - com.packt.camel.chapter3 - 1.0.0.SNAPSHOT | Prefixing body ...
2014-09-11 15:25:46,254 | INFO  | 2 - timer://fire | blueprintRoute
  | 84 - org.apache.camel.camel-core - 2.12.3 | Exchange[ExchangePattern:
InOnly, BodyType: String, Body: Prefixed Hello Chapter3]
2014-09-11 15:25:50,542 | INFO  | 0 - timer://fire | PrefixerProcessor
| 87 - com.packt.camel.chapter3 -
1.0.0.SNAPSHOT | Received in message with body Hello Chapter3
2014-09-11 15:25:50,542 | INFO  | 0 - timer://fire |
PrefixerProcessor              | 87 - com.packt.camel.chapter3 -
1.0.0.SNAPSHOT | Prefixing body ...
2014-09-11 15:25:50,543 | INFO  | 0 - timer://fire | MyRoute
  | 84 - org.apache.camel.camel-core - 2.12.3 |
Exchange[ExchangePattern: InOnly, BodyType: String, Body: Prefixed
Hello Chapter3]
2014-09-11 15:25:50,543 | INFO  | 0 - timer://fire | MyRoute
  | 84 - org.apache.camel.camel-core - 2.12.3 | Exchange[ExchangePattern:
InOnly, BodyType: String, Body: Hello
Chapter3]
2014-09-11 15:25:51,253 | INFO  | 2 - timer://fire |
PrefixerProcessor              | 87 - com.packt.camel.chapter3 -
1.0.0.SNAPSHOT | Received in message with body Hello Chapter3
2014-09-11 15:25:51,254 | INFO  | 2 - timer://fire |
PrefixerProcessor              | 87 - com.packt.camel.chapter3 -
1.0.0.SNAPSHOT | Prefixing body ...
```

```
2014-09-11 15:25:51,254 | INFO  | 2 - timer://fire | blueprintRoute
  | 84 - org.apache.camel.camel-core - 2.12.3 | Exchange[ExchangePattern:
InOnly, BodyType: String, Body: Prefixed
Hello Chapter3]
```

The Camel features also provide Karaf commands that we can use to see the running Camel Contexts and routes.

For instance, the `camel:context-list` command shows the available Camel Contexts, which are as follows:

```
karaf@root()> camel:context-list
 Context        Status        Uptime

 -------        ------        ------

 87-camel-4     Started       7 minutes

 camel-1        Started       7 minutes
```

Here, we can see the two Camel Contexts that we create in our bundle.

We can have details on each Camel Context using the `camel:context-info` command, as follows:

```
karaf@root()> camel:context-info camel-1
Camel Context camel-1
        Name: camel-1
        ManagementName: camel-1
        Version: 2.12.3
        Status: Started
        Uptime: 12 minutes


Statistics
        Exchanges Total: 148
        Exchanges Completed: 148
        Exchanges Failed: 0
        Min Processing Time: 0ms
        Max Processing Time: 8ms
        Mean Processing Time: 2ms
        Total Processing Time: 307ms
        Last Processing Time: 2ms
        Delta Processing Time: 0ms
        Load Avg: 0.00, 0.00, 0.00
```

```
    Reset Statistics Date: 2014-09-11 15:25:04
    First Exchange Date: 2014-09-11 15:25:05
    Last Exchange Completed Date: 2014-09-11 15:37:20
    Number of running routes: 1
    Number of not running routes: 0

Miscellaneous
    Auto Startup: true
    Starting Routes: false
    Suspended: false
    Shutdown timeout: 300 sec.
    Allow UseOriginalMessage: true
    Message History: true
    Tracing: false


Properties


Advanced
    ClassResolver: org.apache.camel.impl.DefaultClassResolver@a44950b
    PackageScanClassResolver: org.apache.camel.impl.DefaultPackageScanC
lassResolver@1c950a71
    ApplicationContextClassLoader: org.apache.camel.camel-core [84]


Components
    timer
    log


Dataformats


Routes
    route1
```

We can see that the `camel-1` context contains one route named `route1`.

Actually, `camel-1` is the Camel Context that we created in the Activator, and `route1` is the route using the Camel Java DSL. Here, we are able to see `CamelContext`, thanks to the OSGi service registration that we perform in the Activator.

On the other hand, we have another Camel Context named 87-camel-4, which is as follows:

```
karaf@root()> camel:context-info 87-camel-4
Camel Context 87-camel-4
      Name: 87-camel-4
      ManagementName: 87-87-camel-4
      Version: 2.12.3
      Status: Started
      Uptime: 15 minutes


Statistics
      Exchanges Total: 188
      Exchanges Completed: 188
      Exchanges Failed: 0
      Min Processing Time: 0ms
      Max Processing Time: 2ms
      Mean Processing Time: 1ms
      Total Processing Time: 264ms
      Last Processing Time: 1ms
      Delta Processing Time: 0ms
      Load Avg: 0.00, 0.00, 0.00
      Reset Statistics Date: 2014-09-11 15:25:05
      First Exchange Date: 2014-09-11 15:25:06
      Last Exchange Completed Date: 2014-09-11 15:40:41
      Number of running routes: 1
      Number of not running routes: 0


Miscellaneous
      Auto Startup: true
      Starting Routes: false
      Suspended: false
      Shutdown timeout: 300 sec.
      Allow UseOriginalMessage: true
      Message History: true
      Tracing: false
```

```
Properties


Advanced
     ClassResolver: org.apache.camel.core.osgi.
OsgiClassResolver@60e8b22b
     PackageScanClassResolver: org.apache.camel.core.osgi.OsgiPackageSca
nClassResolver@4d0956c1
     ApplicationContextClassLoader: BundleDelegatingClassLoader(com.
packt.camel.chapter3 [87])


Components
     timer
     properties
     log


Dataformats


Routes
     route2
```

In this Camel Context (the one created by Camel as declared in the Blueprint descriptor), we can see `route2` corresponding to the route described using the Camel Blueprint DSL.

We can also obtain details about the routes using the `camel:route-info` command (the `camel:route-list` command displays the list of all routes for all Camel Contexts):

```
karaf@root()> camel:route-list
 Context        Route          Status

 -------        -----          ------

 87-camel-4     route2         Started
 camel-1        route1         Started
```

We can take a look at the details for `route1` in the following code:

```
karaf@root()> camel:route-info route1
Camel Route route1
     Camel Context: camel-1
```

Properties

        id = route1

        parent = 31b3f7f4

        group = com.packt.camel.chapter3.MyRouteBuilder

Statistics

    Inflight Exchanges: 0

    Exchanges Total: 382

    Exchanges Completed: 382

    Exchanges Failed: 0

    Min Processing Time: 0 ms

    Max Processing Time: 8 ms

    Mean Processing Time: 1 ms

    Total Processing Time: 674 ms

    Last Processing Time: 2 ms

    Delta Processing Time: 0 ms

    Load Avg: 0.00, 0.00, 0.00

    Reset Statistics Date: 2014-09-11 15:25:04

    First Exchange Date: 2014-09-11 15:25:05

    Last Exchange Completed Date: 2014-09-11 15:56:50

Definition

```xml
<?xml version="1.0" encoding="UTF-8" standalone="yes"?>
<route group="com.packt.camel.chapter3.MyRouteBuilder" id="route1"
  xmlns="http://camel.apache.org/schema/spring">
  <from uri="timer:fire?period=5000"/>
  <setBody id="setBody1">
      <expressionDefinition>Hello Chapter3</expressionDefinition>
  </setBody>
  <process id="process1"/>
  <to uri="log:MyRoute" id="to1"/>
  <process id="process2"/>
  <to uri="log:MyRoute" id="to2"/>
</route>
```

We can see that the route has been executed 382 times without errors. We can also see a dump of the route with the two processors, coming from MyRouteBuilder.

We can also see the details of `route2` corresponding to the routing described using the Camel Blueprint DSL:

```
karaf@root()> camel:route-info route2
Camel Route route2
    Camel Context: 87-camel-4


Properties
            id = route2
            parent = 465796cf


Statistics
        Inflight Exchanges: 0
        Exchanges Total: 414
        Exchanges Completed: 414
        Exchanges Failed: 0
        Min Processing Time: 0 ms
        Max Processing Time: 3 ms
        Mean Processing Time: 1 ms
        Total Processing Time: 529 ms
        Last Processing Time: 1 ms
        Delta Processing Time: 0 ms
        Load Avg: 0.00, 0.00, 0.00
        Reset Statistics Date: 2014-09-11 15:25:05
        First Exchange Date: 2014-09-11 15:25:06
        Last Exchange Completed Date: 2014-09-11 15:59:31


Definition
<?xml version="1.0" encoding="UTF-8" standalone="yes"?>
<route id="route2" xmlns="http://camel.apache.org/schema/spring">
  <from uri="timer:fire?period=5000"/>
  <setBody id="setBody2">
      <constant>Hello Chapter3</constant>
  </setBody>
  <process ref="prefixerProcessor" id="process3"/>
  <to uri="log:blueprintRoute" id="to3"/>
</route>
```

Summary

Processor is one of the most important components of Camel. It's like a Swiss knife. You can use processor to implement message translation and transformation, and any kind of EIPs. All Camel EIPs are implemented using processor to implement the Camel component using `ProcessorEndpoint`. We will see later that processors are also useful for error handling or for unit tests. To make it even easier, you can also use existing beans, acting as processors. Camel can directly use your existing beans thanks to an extended bean support, as we will see in the next chapter.

4
Beans

In the previous chapter, we saw one of the key, and very helpful, Camel components — the processor. However, a processor is tied to Camel as it extends the `org.apache.camel.Processor` interface.

This means that in order to reuse some existing beans in your application, you have to wrap it in a processor, meaning additional code to be maintained.

Fortunately, Camel has extensive support for POJO and beans, and bean model frameworks such as Spring or Blueprint.

In this chapter, we will see:

- How Camel looks for beans in different registries and the different registry implementations
- How Camel acts as a service activator to load the beans and bind the parameters
- The Camel annotations that enables *advanced* binding
- The Camel language annotations that allow the usage of code in parameter binding

Registry

It's possible to use a bean exactly as a processor, meaning, directly inline in a route. This allows us to use a lightweight, simple programming model, reusing existing components in Camel routes.

When a bean is used in a Camel route, the bean must be registered in a registry. Depending on which environment is running, Camel bootstraps different registries. When Camel works with beans, it looks them up in the registry to locate them.

The registry is defined at the CamelContext level. A registry is automatically created for you by Camel with the CamelContext. If you create the CamelContext manually, you can instantiate a registry and put this registry in the CamelContext.

The following registry implementations are shipped with Camel:

- SimpleRegistry
- JndiRegistry
- ApplicationContextRegistry
- OsgiServiceRegistry

Let's have a look at each one of these in detail.

SimpleRegistry

SimpleRegistry is a simple implementation, mostly used for testing where only a limited number of JDK classes are available. It's basically a simple Map.

You have to create an instance of SimpleRegistry by hand before using it. Camel doesn't load any SimpleRegistry by default.

The following example in (chapter4a folder) shows how to create a SimpleRegistry, register a bean, and use it in a Camel route.

In this example, we instantiate a SimpleRegistry that we put in a CamelContext that we create as well.

We populate the SimpleRegistry with a SimpleBean.

In the CamelContext, we add a route that calls the SimpleBean.

To simplify the execution, we embed this code in a main method that we execute via a Maven plugin.

The Maven pom.xml is the following:

```
<?xml version="1.0" encoding="UTF-8"?>
<project xmlns="http://maven.apache.org/POM/4.0.0"
xmlns:xsi="http://www.w3.org/2001/XMLSchema-instance"
xsi:schemaLocation="http://maven.apache.org/POM/4.0.0
http://maven.apache.org/xsd/maven-4.0.0.xsd">

    <modelVersion>4.0.0</modelVersion>

    <groupId>com.packt.camel</groupId>
    <artifactId>chapter4a</artifactId>
```

```
<version>1.0-SNAPSHOT</version>
<packaging>jar</packaging>

<dependencies>
    <dependency>
        <groupId>org.apache.camel</groupId>
        <artifactId>camel-core</artifactId>
        <version>2.12.4</version>
    </dependency>
</dependencies>

<build>
    <plugins>
        <plugin>
            <groupId>org.codehaus.mojo</groupId>
            <artifactId>exec-maven-plugin</artifactId>
            <version>1.3.2</version>
            <executions>
                <execution>
                    <id>launch</id>
                    <phase>verify</phase>
                    <goals>
                        <goal>java</goal>
                    </goals>
                    <configuration>
                        <mainClass>com.packt.camel.chapter4a.
Main</mainClass>
                    </configuration>
                </execution>
            </executions>
        </plugin>
    </plugins>
</build>

</project>
```

In the `src/main/java` folder of the project, we create the `com.packt.camel.chapter4a` package.

In this package, we have:

- A `SimpleBean` class
- A `Main` class

The `SimpleBean` class is pretty simple; it just says hello:

```
package com.packt.camel.chapter4a;

public class SimpleBean {

    public String hello(String message) {
        System.out.println("***** Hello " + message + " *****");
        return "Hello" + message;
    }

}
```

The `Main` class contains only the main method. It's in this method that:

- We create a `SimpleRegistry`
- We populate the registry with an instance of the `SimpleBean`
- We create a `CamelContext`, which uses our `SimpleRegistry`
- We create and add a route in the `CamelContext`. This route uses the `SimpleBean` from the registry

Here's the code:

```
package com.packt.camel.chapter4a;

import org.apache.camel.CamelContext;
import org.apache.camel.ProducerTemplate;
import org.apache.camel.builder.RouteBuilder;
import org.apache.camel.impl.DefaultCamelContext;
import org.apache.camel.impl.SimpleRegistry;

public final class Main {

  public static void main(String[] args) throws Exception {
    SimpleRegistry registry = new SimpleRegistry();
    registry.put("simpleBean", new SimpleBean());

    CamelContext camelContext = new DefaultCamelContext(registry);
    camelContext.addRoutes(new RouteBuilder() {
      @Override
      public void configure() throws Exception {

from("direct:start").to("bean:simpleBean").to("mock:stop");
        }
      }
```

```
        );

      camelContext.start();

        ProducerTemplate producerTemplate =
      camelContext.createProducerTemplate();
        producerTemplate.sendBody("direct:start", "Packt");
        camelContext.stop();
        }
     }
```

To run the project, use the following command:

`mvn clean install`

You should see the execution:

```
[INFO] --- exec-maven-plugin:1.3.2:java (launch) @ chapter4a ---
Hello Packt
[INFO]
```

This proves that the `SimpleRegistry` has been used by our `CamelContext`. Camel succeeded in looking for the bean in the registry and using it.

JndiRegistry

`JndiRegistry` is an implementation that uses an existing **Java Naming and Directory (JNDI)** registry to look up beans. It's the default registry used by Camel when using the Camel Java DSL.

A `JndiRegistry` can be constructed using a JNDI InitialContext. It gives the flexibility to use existing JNDI InitialContext. Camel itself provides a simple `JndiContext` that you can use with the `JndiRegistry`.

We can illustrate the usage of a `JndiRegistry` by implementing an example very similar to the previous one (using a `SimpleRegistry`).

The Maven `pom.xml` is basically the same as in the previous example:

```xml
<?xml version="1.0" encoding="UTF-8"?>
<project xmlns="http://maven.apache.org/POM/4.0.0"
xmlns:xsi="http://www.w3.org/2001/XMLSchema-instance"
xsi:schemaLocation="http://maven.apache.org/POM/4.0.0
http://maven.apache.org/xsd/maven-4.0.0.xsd">

   <modelVersion>4.0.0</modelVersion>
```

```
<groupId>com.packt.camel</groupId>
<artifactId>chapter4b</artifactId>
<version>1.0-SNAPSHOT</version>
<packaging>jar</packaging>

<dependencies>
    <dependency>
        <groupId>org.apache.camel</groupId>
        <artifactId>camel-core</artifactId>
        <version>2.12.4</version>
    </dependency>
</dependencies>

<build>
    <plugins>
        <plugin>
            <groupId>org.codehaus.mojo</groupId>
            <artifactId>exec-maven-plugin</artifactId>
            <version>1.3.2</version>
            <executions>
                <execution>
                    <id>launch</id>
                    <phase>verify</phase>
                    <goals>
                        <goal>java</goal>
                    </goals>
                    <configuration>
                        <mainClass>com.packt.camel.chapter4b.Main</mainClass>
                    </configuration>
                </execution>
            </executions>
        </plugin>
    </plugins>
</build>

</project>
```

In the `src/main/java` directory of the project, we create the
`com.packt.camel.chapter4b` package.

This package contains a `SimpleBean` class similar to the one in the previous example:

```
package com.packt.camel.chapter4b;

public class SimpleBean {

  public String hello(String message) {
    System.out.println("Hello " + message);
    return "Hello" + message;
  }
}
```

Finally, the main difference is in the `Main` class; we just replace the `SimpleRegistry` with a `JndiRegistry`:

```
package com.packt.camel.chapter4b;

import org.apache.camel.CamelContext;
import org.apache.camel.ProducerTemplate;
import org.apache.camel.builder.RouteBuilder;
import org.apache.camel.impl.DefaultCamelContext;
import org.apache.camel.impl.JndiRegistry;
import org.apache.camel.util.jndi.JndiContext;

public final class Main {

  public static void main(String[] args) throws Exception {
    JndiRegistry registry = new JndiRegistry(new JndiContext());
    registry.bind("simpleBean", new SimpleBean());

    CamelContext camelContext = new DefaultCamelContext(registry);
    camelContext.addRoutes(new RouteBuilder() {
      @Override
      public void configure() throws Exception {
from("direct:start").to("bean:simpleBean").to("mock:stop");
      }
    }
    );

  camelContext.start();

    ProducerTemplate producerTemplate =
camelContext.createProducerTemplate();
```

```
        producerTemplate.sendBody("direct:start", "Packt");

        camelContext.stop();
    }
}
```

To run the project, use the following command:

```
mvn clean install
```

The execution gives basically the same result:

```
[INFO] --- exec-maven-plugin:1.3.2:java (launch) @ chapter4b ---
[WARNING] Warning: killAfter is now deprecated. Do you need it ?
Please comment on MEXEC-6.
```

```
Hello Packt
```

We switched to another registry implementation without any impact on the execution.

As a reminder, the `JndiRegistry` is implicitly created by Camel when you use the Java DSL for your route.

ApplicationContextRegistry

`ApplicationContextRegistry` is a Spring-based implementation to look up beans from the Spring `ApplicationContext`. This implementation is automatically used when you are using Camel in a Spring environment.

OsgiServiceRegistry

`OsgiServiceRegistry` is a hook to the OSGi Service Registry. It's used by Camel when running in OSGi environment.

Creating CompositeRegistry

These registries can be composed to create a multilayer registry using a `CompositeRegistry`.

You can create a `CompositeRegistry` by adding other registries.

To illustrate the usage of a `CompositeRegistry`, we create a new example.

Again, the Maven `pom.xml` is basically the same:

```xml
<?xml version="1.0" encoding="UTF-8"?>
<project xmlns="http://maven.apache.org/POM/4.0.0"
xmlns:xsi="http://www.w3.org/2001/XMLSchema-instance"
xsi:schemaLocation="http://maven.apache.org/POM/4.0.0
http://maven.apache.org/xsd/maven-4.0.0.xsd">

    <modelVersion>4.0.0</modelVersion>

    <groupId>com.packt.camel</groupId>
    <artifactId>chapter4c</artifactId>
    <version>1.0-SNAPSHOT</version>
    <packaging>jar</packaging>

    <dependencies>
        <dependency>
            <groupId>org.apache.camel</groupId>
            <artifactId>camel-core</artifactId>
            <version>2.12.4</version>
        </dependency>
    </dependencies>

    <build>
        <plugins>
            <plugin>
                <groupId>org.codehaus.mojo</groupId>
                <artifactId>exec-maven-plugin</artifactId>
                <version>1.3.2</version>
                <executions>
                    <execution>
                        <id>launch</id>
                        <phase>verify</phase>
                        <goals>
                            <goal>java</goal>
                        </goals>
                        <configuration>
                            <mainClass>com.packt.camel.chapter4c.
Main</mainClass>
                        </configuration>
                    </execution>
                </executions>
            </plugin>
```

```
            </plugins>
        </build>
    </project>
```

In the `src/main/java` directory of the project, we have a `com.packt.camel.chapter4c` package.

We again have the sample `SimpleBean` class:

```
package com.packt.camel.chapter4c;

public class SimpleBean {

    public static String hello(String message) {
        System.out.println("Hello " + message);
        return "Hello" + message;
    }
}
```

But this time, in the `Main` class, we create two registries that we gather in a composite registry.

To illustrate the usage, we create two instances of the `SimpleBean` in each registry part of the composite, each instance having a different name in the registries.

We now create two routes in the `CamelContext`; one route uses the `SimpleBean` instance, and the other uses the `otherBean` instance:

```
package com.packt.camel.chapter4c;

import org.apache.camel.CamelContext;
import org.apache.camel.ProducerTemplate;
import org.apache.camel.builder.RouteBuilder;
import org.apache.camel.impl.CompositeRegistry;
import org.apache.camel.impl.DefaultCamelContext;
import org.apache.camel.impl.JndiRegistry;
import org.apache.camel.impl.SimpleRegistry;
import org.apache.camel.util.jndi.JndiContext;

public final class Main {

  public static void main(String[] args) throws Exception {
    SimpleRegistry simpleRegistry = new SimpleRegistry();
    simpleRegistry.put("simpleBean", new SimpleBean());
    JndiRegistry jndiRegistry = new JndiRegistry(new
JndiContext());
```

```
        jndiRegistry.bind("otherBean", new SimpleBean());
        CompositeRegistry registry = new CompositeRegistry();
        registry.addRegistry(simpleRegistry);
        registry.addRegistry(jndiRegistry);

        CamelContext camelContext = new DefaultCamelContext(registry);
        camelContext.addRoutes(new RouteBuilder() {
          @Override
          public void configure() throws Exception {

    from("direct:start").to("bean:simpleBean").to("mock:stop");

    from("direct:other").to("bean:otherBean").to("mock:stop");
          }
        }
        );

        camelContext.start();

        ProducerTemplate producerTemplate =
    camelContext.createProducerTemplate();
        producerTemplate.sendBody("direct:start", "Packt");
        producerTemplate.sendBody("direct:other", "Other");

        camelContext.stop();
      }
    }
```

To run the project, use the following command:

```
mvn clean install
```

Now, at execution time, we can see that the two routes have been executed, each route using the bean instance in the registry. But actually, each instance is in a different registry:

```
[INFO] --- exec-maven-plugin:1.3.2:java (launch) @ chapter4c ---
[WARNING] Warning: killAfter is now deprecated. Do you need it ?
Please comment on MEXEC-6.



Hello Packt
Hello Other
```

Service activator

Camel acts as a service activator, using `BeanProcessor`, which sits between the caller and the actual bean.

The `BeanProcessor` is a special processor that converts the inbound exchange to a method invocation on a bean (POJO).

The `BeanProcessor` performs the following steps when called:

1. It looks up the bean in the registry.
2. It selects the method to invoke the bean.
3. It binds to the parameters of the selected method.
4. It actually invokes the method.
5. It possibly handles any invocation errors that occurred.
6. It sets the method's reply as the body of the output message.

Bean and method bindings

During step 2, when the `BeanProcessor` selects the method to invoke, the message/method bindings can occur in different ways. Camel tries the following steps to resolve the bean method:

1. If the incoming message (`in` message) contains the `CamelBeanMethodName` header, then this method is invoked, converting the `in` message body to the type of the method's argument.
2. You can specify the method name directly in the route definition (on the bean endpoint).
3. If the bean contains a method annotated with `@Handler`, then this method is invoked.
4. If the bean can be converted to a processor (containing the `process()` method), we fall back to the regular processor usage as seen in the previous chapter.
5. If the body of the `in` message can be converted to a `org.apache.camel.component.bean.BeanInvocation` component, then it's the result of the `getMethod()` method, which is used as the method name.
6. Otherwise, the body type of the `in` message is used to find a matching method.

Several exceptions can occur during the method lookup. They are as follows:

- If Camel cannot find the method, it throws a `MethodNotFoundException` exception

- If Camel cannot uniquely resolve a method (for instance, depending on the method argument), it throws an `AmbigiousMethodCallException` exception.

- Before Camel invokes the selected method, it must convert the in message body to the parameter type required by the method. If this fails, a `NoTypeConversionAvailableException` exception is thrown.

Once the method name has been identified, Camel populates the method parameters; it's what we name method parameters binding.

Some Camel types are automatically bound, such as:

- `org.apache.camel.Exchange`
- `org.apache.camel.Message`
- `org.apache.camel.CamelContext`
- `org.apache.camel.TypeConverter`
- `org.apache.camel.spi.Registry`
- `java.lang.Exception`

It means that you can directly use any of these types in the method parameters.

For instance, your bean may contain a single method:

```
public void doMyStuff(Exchange exchange);
```

Camel will provide the current exchange to your method.

By default, Camel will try to convert the in message body as the first parameter of the method.

The return statement of the bean method is used to populate the body of the in message (in case the bean is used via the Camel bean component) or a header value (in case the bean is used via the setHeader Camel statement).

However, depending on your bean, you might have some ambiguity. Camel gives you fine-grained control of the method parameters by providing a set of annotations, which we will cover in the following section.

Annotations

Depending on your bean, you might have some ambiguity. Camel gives you fine-grained control of the method parameters by providing a set of annotations.

Thanks to the annotations, you can describe the expected binding for both method binding and parameter binding.

For method binding, Camel provides the `@Handler` annotation. This annotation allows you to specify the method that Camel will use during execution.

For instance, you may have the following bean:

```
public class MyBean {
   public void other(String class) {   }

public void doMyStuff(String class) { ... }
}
```

In that case, Camel (without specifying the method to use in the route definition) will fail to find the method to call.

The `@Handler` annotation removes the ambiguity:

```
public class MyBean {
   public void other(String class) { … }
   @Handler
public void doMyStuff(String class) { ... }
}
```

Camel also provides annotations for the method parameters binding. The `@Body` binds the parameter to the `in` message body. It allows to bind type like directly a POJO:

```
@Handler
public void doMyLogic(@Body MyPojo pojo) { … }
```

Camel will use a converter to transform the actual in message body to the expected type of the method parameter. The `@ExchangeException` binds the parameter to the `Exchange` exception. This annotation allows you to directly inject the `Exchange` exception in your method. For instance, you can test if the exception is not null and react accordingly.

```
public void doMyLogic(@Body String body, @ExchangeException
Exception exception) {
   if (exception != null) { … } else { … }
}
```

The `@Header` binds the parameter to a header of the in message. You can specify the header name on the annotation as follows:

```
public void doMyLogic(@Body String body, @Header("FirstHeader")
String firstHeader, @Header("SecondHeader") String second header)
{ … }
```

The `@Headers` binds the parameter to the `Map` containing all headers of the `in` message. It's especially interesting when you have to manipulate multiple headers in your method. Using this annotation, the parameter has to be of the `Map` type.

```
public void doMyLogic(@Body String body, @Headers Map headers) { …
}
```

On the other hand, like `@Headers` for the in message, the `@OutHeaders` annotation binds the parameter to the `Map` containing all headers of the `out` message. It's especially interesting when you have to populate some headers (using the `put()` method on the Map):

```
public void doMyLogic(@Body String body, @Headers Map inHeaders,
@OutHeaders Map outHeaders) { … }
```

The `@Property` binds a property of the `Exchange`. As a reminder, the lifetime of a property is the `Exchange`, whereas a header is related to a message. The name of the property is directly provided on the annotation.

```
public void doMyLogic(@Body String body, @Property("TheProperty")
String exProperty) { … }
```

As for the headers, `@Properties` binds a property to the `Map` containing all the properties of the `Exchange`. Again, it's interesting to add new properties to the method (using the `put()` method of the `Map`):

```
public void doMyLogic(@Body String body, @Properties Map
exProperties) { … }
```

Annotations for expression languages

It's also possible to directly leverage the languages supported by Camel to populate the method parameters.

The following annotations are provided:

- `@Bean` binds another bean to the parameter. It allows you to inject a bean into a bean. Camel will look for the bean with the ID provided in the annotation:

  ```
  public void doMyLogic(@Body String body,
  @Bean("anotherBean") AnotherBean anotherBean) { … }
  ```

- `@BeanShell` binds the result of a bean method call to the parameter. BeanShell is a convenient language allowing you to explicitly call a bean method. The bean scripting is defined directly on the annotation:

```
public void doMyLogic(@Body String body,
@BeanShell("myBean.thisIsMyMethod()") methodResult) { … }
```

- `@Constant` binds a static String to the parameter:

```
public void doMyLogic(@Body String body, @Constant("It
doesn't change") String myConstant) { … }
```

- `@EL` binds the result of an expression language (JUEL) to the parameter. The expression is defined in the annotation:

```
public void doMyLogic(@Body String body,
@EL("in.header.myHeader == 'expectedValue') boolean
matched) { … }
```

- `@Groovy` binds the result of a Groovy expression to the parameter. The expression is defined in the annotation. The request keyword corresponds to the in message:

```
public void doMyLogic(@Body String body,
@Groovy("request.attribute") String attributeValue) { … }
```

- `@JavaScript` binds the result of a JavaScript expression to the parameter. The expression is defined in the annotation:

```
public void doMyLogic(@Body String body,
@JavaScript(in.headers.get('myHeader') == 'expectedValue')
boolean matched) { … }
```

- `@MVEL` binds the result of a MVEL expression to the parameter. The expression is defined in the annotation. The request keyword corresponds to the in message:

```
public void doMyLogic(@Body String body,
@MVEL("in.headers.myHeader == 'expectedValue'") boolean
matched) { … }
```

- `@OGNL` binds the result of a OGNL expression to the parameter. The expression is defined in the annotation. The request keyword corresponds to the in message:

```
public void doMyLogic(@Body String body,
@OGNL("in.headers.myHeader == 'expectedValue'") boolean
matched) { … }
```

- @PHP binds the result of a PHP expression to the parameter. The expression is defined in the annotation. The request keyword corresponds to the in message:

```
public void doMyLogic(@Body String body,
@PHP("in.headers.myHeader == 'expectedValue'") boolean
matched) { … }
```

- @Python binds the result of a Python expression to the parameter. The expression is defined in the annotation. The request keyword corresponds to the in message:

```
public void doMyLogic(@Body String body,
@Python("in.headers.myHeader == 'expectedValue'") boolean
matched) { … }
```

- @Ruby binds the result of a Ruby expression to the parameter. The expression is defined in the annotation. The request Ruby variable corresponds to the in message:

```
public void doMyLogic(@Body String body,
@Ruby("$request.headers['myHeader'] == 'expectedValue'")
boolean matched) { … }
```

- @Simple binds the result of a simple expression to the parameter. The expression is defined in the annotation. Simple is a Camel language allowing you to define simple expressions directly using the Camel objects:

```
public void doMyLogic(@Body String body,
@Simple("${in.header.myHeader}") String myHeader) { … }
```

- @XPath binds the result of a XPath expression to the parameter. The expression is defined in the annotation. It's very convenient to extract part of an XML in message:

```
public void doMyLogic(@XPath("//person/name") String name)
{ … }
```

- @XQuery binds the result of a XQuery expression to the parameter. The expression is defined in the annotation. Like XPath, it's very convenient to extract part of a XML in message:

```
public void doMyLogic(@XQuery("/person/@name") String name)
{ … }
```

Of course, it's possible to combine the different annotations with multiple parameters.

Camel gives you great flexibility, irrespective of the language that you already know, you can use it in the expressions and predicates definition.

Example – creating an OSGi bundle with a bean

We illustrate the use of beans in a simple example. This example will create an OSGi bundle containing a bean called by a Camel route.

We will create a bean used in two parts of a route:

- One that directly uses the Camel bean component to change the body of the in message
- Another to define a header in the route

First, we create the Maven project pom.xml for our bundle:

```xml
<?xml version="1.0" encoding="UTF-8"?>
<project xmlns="http://maven.apache.org/POM/4.0.0"
xmlns:xsi="http://www.w3.org/2001/XMLSchema-instance"
xsi:schemaLocation="http://maven.apache.org/POM/4.0.0
http://maven.apache.org/xsd/maven-4.0.0.xsd">

  <modelVersion>4.0.0</modelVersion>

  <groupId>com.packt.camel</groupId>
  <artifactId>chapter4</artifactId>
  <version>1.0-SNAPSHOT</version>
  <packaging>bundle</packaging>

  <dependencies>
      <dependency>
          <groupId>org.apache.camel</groupId>
          <artifactId>camel-core</artifactId>
          <version>2.12.4</version>
      </dependency>
  </dependencies>

  <build>
      <plugins>
          <plugin>
              <groupId>org.apache.felix</groupId>
              <artifactId>maven-bundle-plugin</artifactId>
              <version>2.3.7</version>
              <extensions>true</extensions>
              <configuration>
                  <instructions>
```

```
            <Import-Package>*</Import-Package>
        </instructions>
      </configuration>
    </plugin>
  </plugins>
</build>

</project>
```

This `pom.xml` is pretty simple:

- It defines the Camel core dependency in order to get the bean annotations
- It uses the Maven bundle plugin to package the bean and the route as an OSGi bundle

Creating the MyBean class

We create the `MyBean` class containing two methods:

- The `doMyLogic()` method is annotated as `@Handler` as described previously. It's the one that will be used by the Camel Bean component. This method has a unique parameter `body` of the `String` type. Thanks to the `@Body` annotation, this parameter will be populated by Camel with the body of the in message.
- The `setMyHeader()` method just returns `String`. This method will be used by Camel to populate a header of the in message.

The code of `MyBean` class is as follows:

```java
package com.packt.camel.chapter4;

import org.apache.camel.Body;
import org.apache.camel.Handler;

public class MyBean {

  @Handler
  public String doMyLogic(@Body String body) {
      return "My Logic got " + body;
  }

  public String setMyHeader() {
      return "Here's my header definition, whatever the logic is";
  }

}
```

We can note that the doMyLogic() method defines the bean as a message translator: it transforms the body of the in message in another message body. It looks like the `PrefixerProcessor` used in the previous chapter.

Writing a route definition using the Camel Blueprint DSL

We are going to use Blueprint DSL to write the definition of the route. Thanks to this, we don't have to provide all the plumbing code to create the `CamelContext` and reference it as an OSGi service.

The `CamelContext` is implicitly created by Camel, and we describe the route directly using XML.

In the `OSGI-INF/blueprint` folder of our bundle, we create the following `route.xml` definition:

```xml
<?xml version="1.0" encoding="UTF-8"?>
<blueprint xmlns="http://www.osgi.org/xmlns/blueprint/v1.0.0">

  <bean id="myBean" class="com.packt.camel.chapter4.MyBean"/>

  <camelContext xmlns="http://camel.apache.org/schema/blueprint">
      <route>
          <from uri="timer:fire?period=5000"/>
          <setBody><constant>Hello Chapter4</constant></setBody>
          <to uri="bean:myBean"/>
          <setHeader headerName="myHeaderSetByTheBean">
              <method bean="myBean" method="setMyHeader"/>
          </setHeader>
          <to uri="log:blueprintRoute"/>
      </route>
  </camelContext>

</blueprint>
```

First, we declare our bean in the Blueprint container. It means that the Blueprint container will use our class to create an instance of this bean and give it an ID.

When using the Blueprint DSL, Camel uses a Blueprint container registry; this means that Camel will lookup the beans using the ID in the Blueprint container.

Using Camel, DSL would use exactly the same behavior.

The `<route/>` element defines the following route:

1. The route starts with a timer that creates an empty exchange every 5 seconds.

2. We define a static content Hello Chapter4 for the body of the `in` message using `<setBody/>`.

3. The exchange is sent to our bean. We use the Camel Bean component to directly call `myBean`. Camel will look for a bean named myBean in the Blueprint container. Once found, it will use the `doMyLogic()` method as it's the one with the `@Handler` annotation. Camel will bind the body of the in message with the `doMyLogic()` body parameter.

4. After the bean processor, we can see another use of the bean. This time, we use the bean (the same instance) to define the `myHeaderSetByTheBean` header of the in message. Here we use the `<method/>` syntax providing the `myBean` bean ID and the `setMyHeader()` method. Camel will look for the bean with the `myBean` ID in the Blueprint container, and it will call the `setMyHeader()` method. The return value of this method will be used to populate the `myHeaderSetByTheBean` header.

5. Finally, we send the exchange to a log endpoint.

Building and deploying

We are now ready to build our bundle.

Using Maven, we run the following command:

```
$ mvn clean install

[INFO] Scanning for projects...
[INFO]
[INFO] ------------------------------------------------------------------------
[INFO] Building chapter4 1.0-SNAPSHOT
[INFO] ------------------------------------------------------------------------
[INFO]
[INFO] --- maven-clean-plugin:2.4.1:clean (default-clean) @ chapter4 ---
[INFO] Deleting /home/jbonofre/Workspace/sample/chapter4/target
[INFO]
[INFO] --- maven-resources-plugin:2.6:resources (default-resources) @ chapter4 ---
```

[WARNING] Using platform encoding (UTF-8 actually) to copy filtered resources, i.e. build is platform dependent!

[INFO] Copying 1 resource

[INFO]

[INFO] --- maven-compiler-plugin:3.2:compile (default-compile) @ chapter4 ---

[INFO] Changes detected - recompiling the module!

[WARNING] File encoding has not been set, using platform encoding UTF-8, i.e. build is platform dependent!

[INFO] Compiling 1 source file to /home/jbonofre/Workspace/sample/chapter4/target/classes

[INFO]

[INFO] --- maven-resources-plugin:2.6:testResources (default-testResources) @ chapter4 ---

[WARNING] Using platform encoding (UTF-8 actually) to copy filtered resources, i.e. build is platform dependent!

[INFO] skip non existing resourceDirectory /home/jbonofre/Workspace/sample/chapter4/src/test/resources

[INFO]

[INFO] --- maven-compiler-plugin:3.2:testCompile (default-testCompile) @ chapter4 ---

[INFO] No sources to compile

[INFO]

[INFO] --- maven-surefire-plugin:2.17:test (default-test) @ chapter4 ---

[INFO] No tests to run.

[INFO]

[INFO] --- maven-bundle-plugin:2.3.7:bundle (default-bundle) @ chapter4 ---

[INFO]

[INFO] --- maven-install-plugin:2.5.1:install (default-install) @ chapter4 ---

[INFO] Installing /home/jbonofre/Workspace/sample/chapter4/target/chapter4-1.0-SNAPSHOT.jar to /home/jbonofre/.m2/repository/com/packt/camel/chapter4/1.0-SNAPSHOT/chapter4-1.0-SNAPSHOT.jar

[INFO] Installing /home/jbonofre/Workspace/sample/chapter4/pom.xml to /home/jbonofre/.m2/repository/com/packt/camel/chapter4/1.0-SNAPSHOT/chapter4-1.0-SNAPSHOT.pom

[INFO]

```
[INFO] --- maven-bundle-plugin:2.3.7:install (default-install) @
chapter4 ---
[INFO] Installing com/packt/camel/chapter4/1.0-SNAPSHOT/chapter4-1.0-
SNAPSHOT.jar
[INFO] Writing OBR metadata
[INFO] -----------------------------------------------------------------
------
[INFO] BUILD SUCCESS
[INFO] -----------------------------------------------------------------
------
[INFO] Total time: 7.037s
[INFO] Finished at: Sun Nov 30 23:07:59 CET 2014
[INFO] Final Memory: 32M/1343M
[INFO] -----------------------------------------------------------------
------
```

Our bundle is now available in our local Maven repository (by default in the `.m2/repository` folder of the home directory).

We can deploy this bundle in a Karaf OSGi container.

After having started Karaf (with `bin/karaf` script for instance), we add the Camel features using the `feature:repo-add` command:

```
karaf@root()> feature:repo-add camel 2.12.4

Adding feature url mvn:org.apache.camel.karaf/apache-
camel/2.12.4/xml/features
```

We install the camel-blueprint feature:

```
karaf@root()> feature:install -v camel-blueprint
Installing feature camel-blueprint 2.12.4
Installing feature camel-core 2.12.4
Installing feature xml-specs-api 2.2.0
Found installed bundle: org.apache.servicemix.specs.activation-api-
1.1 [64]
Found installed bundle: org.apache.servicemix.specs.stax-api-1.0 [65]
Found installed bundle: org.apache.servicemix.specs.jaxb-api-2.2 [66]
Found installed bundle: stax2-api [67]
Found installed bundle: woodstox-core-asl [68]
Found installed bundle: org.apache.servicemix.bundles.jaxb-impl [69]
Found installed bundle: org.apache.camel.camel-core [70]
```

```
Found installed bundle: org.apache.camel.karaf.camel-karaf-commands
[71]

Found installed bundle: org.apache.camel.camel-blueprint [72]
```

We can now install our bundle and start it:

```
karaf@root()> bundle:install mvn:com.packt.camel/chapter4/1.0-
SNAPSHOT
Bundle ID: 73

karaf@root()> bundle:start 73
```

We can see that our routes are running, since we can see the log messages (using the `log:display` command):

```
karaf@root()> log:display
...
2014-11-30 23:13:52,944 | INFO | 1 - timer://fire |
blueprintRoute                 | 70 - org.apache.camel.camel-core
- 2.12.4 | Exchange[ExchangePattern: InOnly, BodyType: String,
Body: My Logic got Hello Chapter4]
2014-11-30 23:13:57,943 | INFO | 1 - timer://fire |
blueprintRoute                 | 70 - org.apache.camel.camel-core
- 2.12.4 | Exchange[ExchangePattern: InOnly, BodyType: String,
Body: My Logic got Hello Chapter4]
2014-11-30 23:14:02,945 | INFO | 1 - timer://fire |
blueprintRoute                 | 70 - org.apache.camel.camel-core
- 2.12.4 | Exchange[ExchangePattern: InOnly, BodyType: String,
Body: My Logic got Hello Chapter4]
2014-11-30 23:14:07,944 | INFO | 1 - timer://fire |
blueprintRoute                 | 70 - org.apache.camel.camel-core
- 2.12.4 | Exchange[ExchangePattern: InOnly, BodyType: String,
Body: My Logic got Hello Chapter4]
```

We can see our route using the `camel:route-list` command:

```
karaf@root()> camel:route-list
 Context        Route        Status
 -------        -----        ------
 73-camel-3     route1       Started
```

The `camel:route-info` command gives details about our route, as follows:

```
karaf@root()> camel:route-info route1
Camel Route route1
      Camel Context: 73-camel-3
```

Properties

        id = route1

        parent = 58a5a53e

Statistics

    Inflight Exchanges: 0

    Exchanges Total: 32

    Exchanges Completed: 32

    Exchanges Failed: 0

    Min Processing Time: 1 ms

    Max Processing Time: 13 ms

    Mean Processing Time: 2 ms

    Total Processing Time: 92 ms

    Last Processing Time: 3 ms

    Delta Processing Time: 0 ms

    Load Avg: 0.00, 0.00, 0.00

    Reset Statistics Date: 2014-11-30 23:13:36

    First Exchange Date: 2014-11-30 23:13:37

    Last Exchange Completed Date: 2014-11-30 23:16:12

Definition

```xml
<?xml version="1.0" encoding="UTF-8" standalone="yes"?>
<route id="route1" xmlns="http://camel.apache.org/schema/spring">
  <from uri="timer:fire?period=5000"/>
  <setBody id="setBody1">
      <constant>Hello Chapter4</constant>
  </setBody>
  <to uri="bean:myBean" id="to1"/>
  <setHeader headerName="myHeaderSetByTheBean" id="setHeader1">
      <method bean="myBean" method="setMyHeader"></method>
  </setHeader>
  <to uri="log:blueprintRoute" id="to2"/>
</route>
```

Thanks to the bean support, it's possible to easily use an existing code in Camel routes.

Moreover, with the wide range of annotations and the supported languages, you have complete control over the usage of your beans.

Using the DSL used to write the route definition, Camel knows on which system it's running, and so, it loads different bean registry implementations, making it possible to define the bean in a standard way.

The Camel bean support is a great complement to the Camel processors.

If most of the EIPs that we will see in the next chapter are implemented using Camel processors, some EIPs can be implemented using a bean (such as MessageTranslator EIP).

Summary

In this chapter, we have seen how to use beans in Camel routes.

First, we saw the different registries supported, where Camel looks for beans. Specifically, we saw the mapping between the Camel DSL used and the default registry loaded. We saw examples of different registries in action, including the composite registry. For this lookup, Camel acts as a service activator. The example showed how to leverage the Spring or Blueprint service registry.

We also saw the usage of the annotations to qualify the method and arguments binding. Those annotations can be combined with language annotations, allowing a very powerful way to populate method arguments.

In the next chapter, we will see one of the Camel key features—routing and Enterprise Integration Patterns support. We will see ready-to-use processors and DSL implementing different EIPs.

5
Enterprise Integration
Patterns

In previous chapters, we have seen how a processor or a bean can be used to implement behavioral changes on the messages.

However, some of those functions provide ways to implement solutions to common problems and, instead of reimplementing the same function in different routes, we can reuse an existing one. Some of these generic message operations are described in the Enterprise Integration Patterns (EIPs) from Gregor Hohpe and Bobby Woolf (http://www.enterpriseintegrationpatterns.com/).

This chapter will introduce the most used EIPs provided by Camel:

- The messaging systems EIPs
- The messaging channels EIPs
- The message construction EIPs
- The message routing EIPs
- The message transformation EIPs
- The messaging endpoints EIPs
- The system management EIPs

Some of these generic message operations are described in the Enterprise Integration Patterns (EIPs) from Gregor Hohpe and Bobby Woolf. It describes the patterns, Camel provides the implementation.

EIP processors

The purpose of an EIP pattern is to apply a change on the message or create a new message:

- A change on the content of the message itself
- A change on the destination endpoint of the message
- A change on the routing depending on the message
- Creating a new message or exchange

In the previous chapter, we have seen how Camel processors and beans can be used to implement such changes.

To provide support of EIPs, Camel actually provides ready-to-use processors, with the DSL language to directly use those processors.

So, instead of reimplementing your own same processor in multiple routes, you can directly use an EIP processor provided by Camel.

The EIPs are classified in different categories, depending on the change performed on the message and the routing function implemented. We will be covering each category in the following sections.

Messaging systems EIPs

Messaging systems EIPs gather all patterns related to the delivery of messages, which are moving along in the routing logic.

Message Channel

The Message Channel EIP is the generic name for the communication between endpoints in a Camel route.

In the examples of the previous chapters, we used endpoints with the following syntax:

```
component:option?key=value&key=value
```

For instance, we can have a route as follows:

```
<from uri="timer:fire?period=5000"/>
<to uri="log:myLog"/>
```

This route uses two endpoints (`timer` and `log`). Camel implicitly creates a Message Channel between the two endpoints.

The purpose is to decouple the endpoint producing the message from the application consuming the message.

This EIP is actually used in basically all routes in an implicit way (you don't have to use a special notation to use Message Channel, it's in Camel).

Message

Another implicit EIP in Camel is the Message EIP.

This EIP is basically implemented by the Camel message interface and wrapped in an exchange.

This EIP is used in combination with the Message Channel one—the message channel transports messages.

Thanks to the Exchange message wrapper, Camel implements the whole Message EIP, including support of the message exchange patterns.

In a Camel Exchange, we have the following pattern property:

- If the pattern is set to `InOnly`, Camel implements an event message (a single inbound message)
- If the pattern is set to `InOut`, Camel implements a `request-reply` with an inbound and outbound message

The first endpoint of a Camel route (the `from`) is responsible for the creation of the exchange and hence, the message with the corresponding pattern. Each endpoint defines the expected pattern (and so if one is waiting for an outbound message to return to the client or not).

Pipeline

The purpose of the Pipeline EIP is to apply a series of actions using the message. For that, we move the message through different steps, like in a pipeline.

We can define a pipeline in two ways with Camel:

- The implicit pipeline is what we used in previous chapters. We simply define the steps in the route definition itself.
- The explicit pipeline uses the pipeline DSL syntax.

The implicit pipeline

The implicit pipeline is the default Camel behavior — the route definition containing the chain of different processors and endpoints is actually a pipeline.

To illustrate this, we create an example containing a Camel route written with the Blueprint DSL.

First, we create the following Maven `pom.xml` file:

```xml
<?xml version="1.0" encoding="UTF-8"?>
<project xmlns="http://maven.apache.org/POM/4.0.0"
xmlns:xsi="http://www.w3.org/2001/XMLSchema-instance"
xsi:schemaLocation="http://maven.apache.org/POM/4.0.0
http://maven.apache.org/xsd/maven-4.0.0.xsd">

  <modelVersion>4.0.0</modelVersion>

  <groupId>com.packt.camel</groupId>
  <artifactId>chapter5a</artifactId>
  <version>1.0-SNAPSHOT</version>
  <packaging>bundle</packaging>

  <build>
      <plugins>
          <plugin>
              <groupId>org.apache.felix</groupId>
              <artifactId>maven-bundle-plugin</artifactId>
              <version>2.3.7</version>
              <extensions>true</extensions>
              <configuration>
                  <instructions>
                      <Import-Package>*</Import-Package>
                  </instructions>
              </configuration>
          </plugin>
      </plugins>
  </build>

</project>
```

This `pom.xml` file is very simple — it just packages our route as an OSGi bundle that we will deploy into the Apache Karaf container. In the project, we create two very simple beans that just display a message when they receive the `in` message.

The first bean is named `Step1Bean`:

```
package com.packt.camel.chapter5a;

public class Step1Bean {

  public static void single(String body) {
      System.out.println("STEP 1: " + body);
  }

}
```

The second bean is named `Step2Bean`:

```
package com.packt.camel.chapter5a;

public class Step2Bean {

  public static void single(String body) {
      System.out.println("STEP 2: " + body);
  }

}
```

Finally, we create the Blueprint XML describing the route (in `src/main/resources/OSGI-INF/blueprint/route.xml`):

```
<?xml version="1.0" encoding="UTF-8"?>
<blueprint xmlns="http://www.osgi.org/xmlns/blueprint/v1.0.0">

  <bean id="step1" class="com.packt.camel.chapter5a.Step1Bean"/>

  <bean id="step2" class="com.packt.camel.chapter5a.Step2Bean"/>

  <camelContext xmlns="http://camel.apache.org/schema/blueprint">
      <route>
          <from uri="timer:fire?period=5000"/>
          <setBody>
              <constant>Hello Chapter5a</constant>
          </setBody>
          <bean ref="step1"/>
          <bean ref="step2"/>
```

```
                <to uri="log:pipeline"/>
        </route>
    </camelContext>

</blueprint>
```

We can see the pipeline here; Camel will route the exchange from the timer's endpoint to the `step1` bean, next to the `step2` bean, and finally to the `log` endpoint.

It's an implicit pipeline. We can see the route in action by building and deploying the bundle into Karaf.

To build the bundle packaging both the route and the beans, we simply do:

```
$ mvn clean install
```

We can start a Karaf container as follows:

```
$ bin/karaf
```

```
karaf@root()>
```

We install the `camel-blueprint` support in Karaf:

```
karaf@root()> feature:repo-add camel 2.12.4
Adding feature url mvn:org.apache.camel.karaf/apache-camel/2.12.4/xml/features
karaf@root()> feature:install camel-blueprint
```

We can now install our bundle:

```
karaf@root()> bundle:install -s mvn:com.packt.camel/chapter5a/1.0-SNAPSHOT
Bundle ID: 73
```

Very quickly, we can see the route execution:

```
STEP 1: Hello Chapter5a
STEP 2: Hello Chapter5a
STEP 1: Hello Chapter5a
STEP 2: Hello Chapter5a
STEP 1: Hello Chapter5a
STEP 2: Hello Chapter5a
```

We can note the pipeline behavior where the message flows from the timer endpoint to the different steps of the route execution.

The explicit pipeline

Another way to use the pipeline EIP is by explicitly defining it with the corresponding DSL syntax.

The different steps are defined with the `pipeline` keyword.

To illustrate this, we will create a route exactly like the previous one (a message created by a timer is sent to two beans and a log endpoint) but this time using the `<pipeline/>` element in the route definition.

The Maven `pom.xml` file is similar to the previous one:

```xml
<?xml version="1.0" encoding="UTF-8"?>
<project xmlns="http://maven.apache.org/POM/4.0.0"
xmlns:xsi="http://www.w3.org/2001/XMLSchema-instance"
xsi:schemaLocation="http://maven.apache.org/POM/4.0.0
http://maven.apache.org/xsd/maven-4.0.0.xsd">

  <modelVersion>4.0.0</modelVersion>

  <groupId>com.packt.camel</groupId>
  <artifactId>chapter5b</artifactId>
  <version>1.0-SNAPSHOT</version>
  <packaging>bundle</packaging>

  <build>
    <plugins>
      <plugin>
        <groupId>org.apache.felix</groupId>
        <artifactId>maven-bundle-plugin</artifactId>
        <version>2.3.7</version>
        <extensions>true</extensions>
        <configuration>
          <instructions>
            <Import-Package>*</Import-Package>
          </instructions>
        </configuration>
      </plugin>
    </plugins>
  </build>

</project>
```

We still have our two beans that display the in message. The first bean is as follows:

```
package com.packt.camel.chapter5b;

public class Step1Bean {

  public static void single(String body) {
      System.out.println("STEP 1: " + body);
  }

}
```

The second bean that displays the in message is as follows:

```
package com.packt.camel.chapter5b;

public class Step2Bean {

  public static void single(String body) {
      System.out.println("STEP 2: " + body);
  }

}
```

Only the Blueprint XML describing the route is different:

```
<?xml version="1.0" encoding="UTF-8"?>
<blueprint xmlns="http://www.osgi.org/xmlns/blueprint/v1.0.0">

  <bean id="step1" class="com.packt.camel.chapter5b.Step1Bean"/>

  <bean id="step2" class="com.packt.camel.chapter5b.Step2Bean"/>

  <camelContext xmlns="http://camel.apache.org/schema/blueprint">
      <route>
          <from uri="timer:fire?period=5000"/>
          <setBody>
              <constant>Hello Chapter5b</constant>
          </setBody>
          <pipeline>
              <bean ref="step1"/>
              <bean ref="step2"/>
              <to uri="log:pipeline"/>
          </pipeline>
      </route>
```

```
    </camelContext>

  </blueprint>
```

As we did in the previous example, we build the OSGi bundle using Maven:

```
$ mvn clean install
```

We deploy our bundle in Karaf:

```
$ bin/karaf
karaf@root()> feature:repo-add camel 2.12.4
Adding feature url mvn:org.apache.camel.karaf/apache-
camel/2.12.4/xml/features
karaf@root()> feature:install camel-blueprint
karaf@root()> bundle:install -s mvn:com.packt.camel/chapter5b/1.0-
SNAPSHOT
Bundle ID: 73
```

We can see that the route execution is exactly the same as it is in the previous example:

```
STEP 1: Hello Chapter5b
STEP 2: Hello Chapter5b
STEP 1: Hello Chapter5b
STEP 2: Hello Chapter5b
```

Basically, the routes are exactly the same internally in Camel, only the notation is different.

In most cases, we use the implicit pipeline (default behavior) which allows you to simplify the route definition.

Message router

The Message Router EIP moves a message to different destinations depending on a condition.

The condition is actually a predicate defined using one of the languages supported by Camel (simple, header, xpath, xquery, mvel, ognl, and so on).

The predicate can use any data to implement the condition. If it uses the content of the message itself, we talk about Content Based Router (which we will see later in this chapter).

To illustrate the Message Router EIP, we create a route that will consume files and copy the files to different output folders depending on the file extension.

We directly write this route using the Blueprint DSL to a `route.xml` file:

```xml
<?xml version="1.0" encoding="UTF-8"?>
<blueprint xmlns="http://www.osgi.org/xmlns/blueprint/v1.0.0">

    <camelContext xmlns="http://camel.apache.org/schema/blueprint">
        <route>
            <from uri="file:/tmp/in"/>
            <choice>
                <when>
                    <simple>${file:ext} == 'xml'</simple>
                    <to uri="file:/tmp/out/xml"/>
                </when>
                <when>
                    <simple>${file:ext} == 'txt'</simple>
                    <to uri="file:/tmp/out/txt"/>
                </when>
                <otherwise>
                    <to uri="file:/tmp/out/binaries"/>
                </otherwise>
            </choice>
        </route>
    </camelContext>

</blueprint>
```

We can see the usage of the `<choice/>` element, which is the notation of the Message Router EIP.

In this choice, we define two conditional routings:

- Using the `simple` language, we define the first predicate checking whether the file extension is `.xml`. If so, the message is routed to a file endpoint creating an output file in the `/tmp/out/xml` folder.

- The second condition also uses the simple language. This predicate checks whether the file extension is `.txt`. If so, the message is routed to a file endpoint creating an output file in the `/tmp/out/txt` folder.

If the two first conditions are not matched, the message is routed to a file endpoint creating an output file in the `/tmp/out/binaries` folder. We start Karaf and install the `camel-blueprint` support:

```
$ bin/karaf

karaf@root()> feature:repo-add camel 2.12.4

Adding feature url mvn:org.apache.camel.karaf/apache-camel/2.12.4/xml/features

karaf@root()> feature:install camel-blueprint
```

We can now simply drop the `route.xml` file in the Karaf `deploy` folder.

In the `/tmp/in` folder, we create three files.

The first file is `file.xml`, which contains :

```
<test>foobar</test>
```

The second file is `file.txt`, which contains :

```
Foobar
```

The third file is `file.csv`, which contains :

```
foo,bar
```

We can see in the `/tmp/out` directory that the three folders have been created and they contain the expected files:

```
/tmp/out$ tree
.
├── binaries
│   └── test.csv
├── txt
│   └── file.txt
└── xml
    └── file.xml
```

Message Translator

The Message Translator EIP is basically the transformation of the message content.

Some steps of the route change the content of the message.

In Camel, you have three ways to implement a message translator:

- You can use the transform DSL notation to call any language supported by Camel

- If the purpose of the translator is to convert from one data format to another, you can use the marshalling/unmarshalling functions provided by Camel

- If you want complete control and implement complex transformation, you can use your own processor or bean to implement the transformation logic

The transform notation

It's possible to use any language supported by Camel (`simple`, `ruby`, `groovy`, and so on) in the `transform` keyword.

The external language is used to apply a transformation on the message.

To illustrate the usage of the transform notation, we can create a Camel route using the following Blueprint descriptor:

```
<?xml version="1.0" encoding="UTF-8"?>
<blueprint xmlns="http://www.osgi.org/xmlns/blueprint/v1.0.0">

  <camelContext xmlns="http://camel.apache.org/schema/blueprint">
      <route>
          <from uri="file:/tmp/in"/>
          <transform>
             <simple>Hello ${in.body}</simple>
          </transform>
          <to uri="file:/tmp/out"/>
      </route>
  </camelContext>

</blueprint>
```

This Camel route uses a Message Translator EIP to prepend `Hello` to the body of the in message.

The route consumes files from the `/tmp/in` folder (thanks to the `from` file endpoint), uses the transform notation with the simple language, and writes the message to a file in the `/tmp/out` folder (thanks to the `to` file endpoint).

We start Karaf and install the `camel-blueprint` feature:

```
$ bin/karaf
karaf@root()> feature:repo-add camel 2.12.4
```

```
Adding feature url mvn:org.apache.camel.karaf/apache-
camel/2.12.4/xml/features
```

`karaf@root()> feature:install camel-blueprint`

We just drop the Blueprint XML file in the Karaf `deploy` folder. We create the `test.txt` file in the `/tmp/in` folder, only containing:

`World`

The Camel route creates a `test.txt` file in the `/tmp/out` folder, containing:

`Hello World`

We can note that the Message Translator EIP changed the body of the `in` message (from `World` to `Hello World`).

Using processor or bean

In previous chapters, we have already used a Camel processor or a bean to change the body of the `in` message.

We perform the same task as we did in the previous example using a processor.

This time, a simple Blueprint XML file is not enough, we have to package the Blueprint XML and the processor in an OSGi bundle.

We create the following Maven `pom.xml` file:

```xml
<?xml version="1.0" encoding="UTF-8"?>
<project xmlns="http://maven.apache.org/POM/4.0.0"
xmlns:xsi="http://www.w3.org/2001/XMLSchema-instance"
xsi:schemaLocation="http://maven.apache.org/POM/4.0.0
http://maven.apache.org/xsd/maven-4.0.0.xsd">

  <modelVersion>4.0.0</modelVersion>

  <groupId>com.packt.camel</groupId>
  <artifactId>chapter5e</artifactId>
  <version>1.0-SNAPSHOT</version>
  <packaging>bundle</packaging>

  <dependencies>
    <dependency>
        <groupId>org.apache.camel</groupId>
        <artifactId>camel-core</artifactId>
```

```xml
                    <version>2.12.4</version>
            </dependency>
        </dependencies>

        <build>
            <plugins>
                <plugin>
                    <groupId>org.apache.felix</groupId>
                    <artifactId>maven-bundle-plugin</artifactId>
                    <version>2.3.7</version>
                    <extensions>true</extensions>
                    <configuration>
                        <instructions>
                            <Import-Package>*</Import-Package>
                        </instructions>
                    </configuration>
                </plugin>
            </plugins>
        </build>

    </project>
```

This Maven `pom.xml` file is very simple, it just defined the `camel-core` dependency (required by our Camel processor) and the OSGi bundle packaging.

We create a `PrependProcessor` class:

```java
package com.packt.camel.chapter5e;

import org.apache.camel.Exchange;
import org.apache.camel.Processor;

public class PrependProcessor implements Processor {

  public void process(Exchange exchange) throws Exception {
      String inBody = exchange.getIn().getBody(String.class);
      inBody = "Hello " + inBody;
      exchange.getIn().setBody(inBody);
  }

}
```

This processor is actually the implementation of the Message Translator EIP — it prepends `Hello` to the inbound message.

Finally, we use this processor in a Camel route written using the Blueprint DSL:

```xml
<?xml version="1.0" encoding="UTF-8"?>
<blueprint xmlns="http://www.osgi.org/xmlns/blueprint/v1.0.0">

  <bean id="prependProcessor"
    class="com.packt.camel.chapter5e.PrependProcessor"/>

  <camelContext xmlns="http://camel.apache.org/schema/blueprint">
      <route>
          <from uri="file:/tmp/in"/>
          <process ref="prependProcessor"/>
          <to uri="file:/tmp/out"/>
      </route>
  </camelContext>

</blueprint>
```

We use Maven to build and package our OSGi bundle:

```
$ mvn clean install
```

We start Karaf and install the `camel-blueprint` feature:

```
$ bin/karaf
karaf@root()> feature:repo-add camel 2.12.4
Adding feature url mvn:org.apache.camel.karaf/apache-camel/2.12.4/xml/features
karaf@root()> feature:install camel-blueprint
```

We install our bundle in Karaf:

```
karaf@root()> bundle:install -s mvn:com.packt.camel/chapter5e/1.0-SNAPSHOT
Bundle ID: 73
```

As in the previous example, we will put a `test.txt` file in the `/tmp/in` folder, which contains this:

```
World
```

Then, we can see `/tmp/in/test.txt` containing:

```
Hello World
```

So, we implemented the same Message Translator EIP but this time using
a processor.

A processor or a bean gives you complete control of the Camel Exchange, and allows
you to implement very complex message transformations.

Marshalling/umarshalling

Instead of changing the content of the message itself, the Message Translator EIP can
be used to convert the message from one data format to another.

Camel supports different data formats and provides functions to directly convert
from one data format to another.

To illustrate marshalling and unmarshalling, we create a route that consumes XML
files and unmarshal/marshal the XML messages as JSON messages, which are sent
to another file endpoint.

We use the Camel Blueprint DSL to define the route:

```xml
<?xml version="1.0" encoding="UTF-8"?>
<blueprint xmlns="http://www.osgi.org/xmlns/blueprint/v1.0.0">

  <camelContext xmlns="http://camel.apache.org/schema/blueprint">
      <dataFormats>
          <xmljson id="xmljson"/>
      </dataFormats>
      <route>
          <from uri="file:/tmp/in"/>
          <marshal ref="xmljson"/>
          <to uri="file:/tmp/out"/>
      </route>
  </camelContext>

</blueprint>
```

This route uses the `xmljson` Camel data format. The marshal element is the
implementation of the Message Translator EIP, which converts the message
from XML to JSON.

We start Karaf and install the `camel-blueprint` and `camel-xmljson` features:

```
$ bin/karaf

karaf@root()> feature:repo-add camel 2.12.4
```

```
Adding feature url mvn:org.apache.camel.karaf/apache-
camel/2.12.4/xml/features
```

```
karaf@root()> feature:install camel-blueprint
```

```
karaf@root()> feature:install camel-xmljson
```

We directly drop our `route.xml` in the `deploy` folder.

In the `/tmp/in` folder, we create the following `person.xml` file, containing:

```
<person>
    <name>jbonofre</name>
    <address>My Street, Paris</address>
</person>
```

In the `/tmp/out` folder, we can see a `person.xml` file, containing:

```
{"name":"jbonofre","address":"My Street, Paris"}
```

Our Message Translator EIP has been executed, using marshalling/unmarshalling to different data formats.

Message Endpoint

The Message Endpoint EIP just defines the way an application can produce or consume messages in the routing system. Basically, in Camel, it's directly implemented and described by the `endpoint` interface. An endpoint is created by a component and described by an URI.

Messaging channels EIPs

Messaging Channel EIPs gather all the patterns moving data from one point to another, using a communication channel.

Point To Point Channel

The Point To Point Channel EIP ensures that only one receiver consumes a message.

In Camel, the support of this EIP is dedicated to the components.

Some components are designed to implement and support this EIP.

For instance, this is the case for:

- The SEDA and VM components, for communication between routes
- The JMS component, when working with JMS queues

To illustrate the Point To Point Channel EIP, we create three routes using the Camel Blueprint DSL:

- The first route starts with a timer and produces a message in a JMS queue
- The second and third routes consume messages from the JMS queue

We will see that one message will only be consumed by one consumer route.

We create the following `route.xml` file:

```xml
<?xml version="1.0" encoding="UTF-8"?>
<blueprint xmlns="http://www.osgi.org/xmlns/blueprint/v1.0.0">

  <bean id="amqConnectionFactory"
    class="org.apache.activemq.ActiveMQConnectionFactory">
      <property name="brokerURL" value="vm://broker"/>
  </bean>

  <camelContext xmlns="http://camel.apache.org/schema/blueprint">
      <route>
          <from uri="timer:fire?period=1000"/>
          <setBody>
             <constant>Hello chapter5g</constant>
          </setBody>
          <to uri="jms:queue:input?
           connectionFactory=#amqConnectionFactory"/>
      </route>
      <route>
          <from uri="jms:queue:input?
           connectionFactory=#amqConnectionFactory"/>
          <delay>
              <constant>2000</constant>
          </delay>
          <to uri="log:consumer1"/>
      </route>
      <route>
          <from uri="jms:queue:input?
           connectionFactory=#amqConnectionFactory"/>
```

```
        <delay>
            <constant>2000</constant>
        </delay>
        <to uri="log:consumer2"/>
    </route>
  </camelContext>

</blueprint>
```

We define a JMS connection factory that embeds an Apache ActiveMQ JMS broker. This connection factory is used in different Camel JMS endpoints.

We start a Karaf instance and we install the `camel-blueprint` and `activemq-camel` features:

```
$ bin/karaf

karaf@root()> feature:repo-add camel 2.12.4

Adding feature url mvn:org.apache.camel.karaf/apache-camel/2.12.4/xml/features

karaf@root()> feature:repo-add activemq 5.7.0

Adding feature url mvn:org.apache.activemq/activemq-karaf/5.7.0/xml/features

karaf@root()> feature:install camel-blueprint

karaf@root()> feature:install activemq-camel

Refreshing bundles org.apache.servicemix.bundles.jaxb-impl (69),
org.apache.camel.camel-core (70)
```

We can now directly drop the `route.xml` file into the Karaf `deploy` folder. In the log ($KARAF_HOME/data/log), we can see:

```
2014-12-15 15:25:22,142 | INFO  | sConsumer[input] | consumer2  | 70
- org.apache.camel.camel-core - 2.12.4 | Exchange[ExchangePattern:
InOnly, BodyType: String, Body: Hello chapter5g]

2014-12-15 15:25:23,105 | INFO  | sConsumer[input] | consumer1 | 70 -
org.apache.camel.camel-core - 2.12.4 | Exchange[ExchangePattern:
InOnly, BodyType: String, Body: Hello chapter5g]

2014-12-15 15:25:24,146 | INFO  | sConsumer[input] | consumer2 | 70 -
org.apache.camel.camel-core - 2.12.4 | Exchange[ExchangePattern:
InOnly, BodyType: String, Body: Hello chapter5g]

2014-12-15 15:25:25,107 | INFO  | sConsumer[input] | consumer1 | 70 -
org.apache.camel.camel-core - 2.12.4 | Exchange[ExchangePattern:
InOnly, BodyType: String, Body: Hello chapter5g]

2014-12-15 15:25:26,149 | INFO  | sConsumer[input] | consumer2 | 70 -
org.apache.camel.camel-core - 2.12.4 | Exchange[ExchangePattern:
InOnly, BodyType: String, Body: Hello chapter5g]
```

```
2014-12-15 15:25:27,109 | INFO | sConsumer[input] | consumer1 | 70 -
org.apache.camel.camel-core - 2.12.4 | Exchange[ExchangePattern:
InOnly, BodyType: String, Body: Hello chapter5g]
2014-12-15 15:25:28,151 | INFO | sConsumer[input] | consumer2 | 70 -
org.apache.camel.camel-core - 2.12.4 | Exchange[ExchangePattern:
InOnly, BodyType: String, Body: Hello chapter5g]
```

We can see that each message is consumed by one route, illustrating the Point To Point Channel EIP.

Publish Subscribe Channel

The Publish Subscribe Channel EIP is similar to the Point To Point Channel EIP, but instead of being consumed by only one consumer, each message is consumed by multiple consumers.

The message is duplicated to all consumers.

As in the Point To Point Channel EIP, Camel supports the Publish Subscribe Channel at a component level.

Some components are designed to implement and support this EIP, such as:

- The JMS component when working with JMS topics
- The SEDA/VM components when working with `multipleConsumers=true` on the endpoints

To illustrate this EIP, we update the previous example to use a topic instead of a queue:

```xml
<?xml version="1.0" encoding="UTF-8"?>
<blueprint xmlns="http://www.osgi.org/xmlns/blueprint/v1.0.0">

  <bean id="amqConnectionFactory"
    class="org.apache.activemq.ActiveMQConnectionFactory">
      <property name="brokerURL" value="vm://broker"/>
  </bean>

  <camelContext xmlns="http://camel.apache.org/schema/blueprint">
      <route>
          <from uri="timer:fire?period=1000"/>
          <setBody>
             <constant>Hello chapter5h</constant>
          </setBody>
```

```
            <to uri="jms:topic: input?
             connectionFactory=#amqConnectionFactory"/>
        </route>
        <route>
            <from uri="jms:topic
             :input?connectionFactory=#amqConnectionFactory"/>
            <delay>
                <constant>2000</constant>
            </delay>
            <to uri="log:consumer1"/>
        </route>
        <route>
            <from uri="jms:topic:input?connectionFactory
             =#amqConnectionFactory"/>
            <delay>
                <constant>2000</constant>
            </delay>
            <to uri="log:consumer2"/>
        </route>
    </camelContext>

</blueprint>
```

As we did in the previous example, we start Karaf and install the `camel-blueprint` and `activemq-camel` features:

```
$ bin/karaf

karaf@root()> feature:repo-add camel 2.12.4

Adding feature url mvn:org.apache.camel.karaf/apache-
camel/2.12.4/xml/features

karaf@root()> feature:repo-add activemq 5.7.0

Adding feature url mvn:org.apache.activemq/activemq-
karaf/5.7.0/xml/features

karaf@root()> feature:install camel-blueprint

karaf@root()> feature:install activemq-camel

Refreshing bundles org.apache.servicemix.bundles.jaxb-impl (69),
org.apache.camel.camel-core (70)
```

We drop the `route.xml` directly into the `deploy` folder. Now, we can see the following in the log:

```
2014-12-15 15:47:45,363 | INFO  | sConsumer[input] | consumer1 | 70 -
 org.apache.camel.camel-core - 2.12.4 | Exchange[ExchangePattern:
InOnly, BodyType: String, Body: Hello chapter5h]
```

```
2014-12-15 15:47:45,363 | INFO  | sConsumer[input] | consumer2 | 70 -
org.apache.camel.camel-core - 2.12.4 | Exchange[ExchangePattern:
InOnly, BodyType: String, Body: Hello chapter5h]

2014-12-15 15:47:47,367 | INFO  | sConsumer[input] | consumer2 | 70 -
org.apache.camel.camel-core - 2.12.4 | Exchange[ExchangePattern:
InOnly, BodyType: String, Body: Hello chapter5h]

2014-12-15 15:47:47,367 | INFO  | sConsumer[input] | consumer1 | 70 -
org.apache.camel.camel-core - 2.12.4 | Exchange[ExchangePattern:
InOnly, BodyType: String, Body: Hello chapter5h]

2014-12-15 15:47:49,369 | INFO  | sConsumer[input] | consumer1 | 70 -
org.apache.camel.camel-core - 2.12.4 | Exchange[ExchangePattern:
InOnly, BodyType: String, Body: Hello chapter5h]

2014-12-15 15:47:49,369 | INFO  | sConsumer[input] | consumer2 | 70 -
org.apache.camel.camel-core - 2.12.4 | Exchange[ExchangePattern:
InOnly, BodyType: String, Body: Hello chapter5h]

2014-12-15 15:47:51,371 | INFO  | sConsumer[input] | consumer2  | 70
- org.apache.camel.camel-core - 2.12.4 | Exchange[ExchangePattern:
InOnly, BodyType: String, Body: Hello chapter5h]

2014-12-15 15:47:51,371 | INFO  | sConsumer[input] | consumer1 | 70 -
org.apache.camel.camel-core - 2.12.4 | Exchange[ExchangePattern:
InOnly, BodyType: String, Body: Hello chapter5h]

2014-12-15 15:47:53,373 | INFO  | sConsumer[input] | consumer2 | 70 -
org.apache.camel.camel-core - 2.12.4 | Exchange[ExchangePattern:
InOnly, BodyType: String, Body: Hello chapter5h]

2014-12-15 15:47:53,373 | INFO  | sConsumer[input] | consumer1 | 70 -
org.apache.camel.camel-core - 2.12.4 | Exchange[ExchangePattern:
InOnly, BodyType: String, Body: Hello chapter5h]
```

We can note that each message has been consumed by the two routes (see the timestamps).

Dead Letter Channel

The Dead Letter Channel EIP allows you to reroute a message to another destination when the actual destination delivery fails.

This EIP is related to the management of errors in Camel routes.

Camel uses extensive support for error management, thanks to different error handlers and policies. We will see error handlers and hence, the Dead Letter Channel EIP, in *Chapter 7, Error Handling*.

Guaranteed Delivery

Guaranteed Delivery ensures that we don't lose any message. It means basically that the messages are persistent and stored in a persistent store.

It allows you to create some checkpoints in your route—if a route stops, the messages are stored. As soon as the route restarts, the *pending* messages are processed.

Camel, by itself, doesn't provide storage for messages, but you can use endpoints allowing the storage of the messages, as follows:

- File endpoints, where the messages are produced as files on the filesystem by a route, and consumed by routes. The store is actually the filesystem.
- JMS endpoints, where the messages (flagged as durable messages) are added into a JMS queue by a route, and consumed by other routes. The message store is actually the broker persistent messages store.
- JPA endpoints, where the messages are produced and stored in a database, and other routes poll the database. The message store is actually the database.

We can illustrate this EIP using two routes sharing a directory on the filesystem to store the messages.

The purpose is to see that, even if the second route is stopped, the messages are persistent and taken by the route as soon as it's started again.

We create a first `route1.xml` file, containing:

```xml
<?xml version="1.0" encoding="UTF-8"?>
<blueprint xmlns="http://www.osgi.org/xmlns/blueprint/v1.0.0">

  <camelContext xmlns="http://camel.apache.org/schema/blueprint">
      <route>
          <from uri="timer:fire?period=1000"/>
          <setBody>
             <constant>Hello chapter5i</constant>
          </setBody>
          <to uri="file:/tmp/exchange"/>
      </route>
  </camelContext>

</blueprint>
```

We start Karaf and install the `camel-blueprint` feature:

```
$ bin/karaf

karaf@root()> feature:repo-add camel 2.12.4

Adding feature url mvn:org.apache.camel.karaf/apache-
camel/2.12.4/xml/features

karaf@root()> feature:install camel-blueprint
```

We drop the `route1.xml` into the `deploy` folder. We can see the first files coming into the `/tmp/exchange` folder:

```
$ /tmp/exchange$ ls -l

total 16

-rw-rw-r-- 1 jbonofre jbonofre 15 Dec 15 16:21 ID-latitude-51643-
1418656861977-0-1

-rw-rw-r-- 1 jbonofre jbonofre 15 Dec 15 16:21 ID-latitude-51643-
1418656861977-0-3

-rw-rw-r-- 1 jbonofre jbonofre 15 Dec 15 16:21 ID-latitude-51643-
1418656861977-0-5

-rw-rw-r-- 1 jbonofre jbonofre 15 Dec 15 16:21 ID-latitude-51643-
1418656861977-0-7
```

Now, we create a `route2.xml` file, containing:

```xml
<?xml version="1.0" encoding="UTF-8"?>
<blueprint xmlns="http://www.osgi.org/xmlns/blueprint/v1.0.0">

  <camelContext xmlns="http://camel.apache.org/schema/blueprint">
    <route>
      <from uri="file:/tmp/exchange"/>
        <convertBodyTo type="java.lang.String"/>
      <to uri="log:route2"/>
    </route>
  </camelContext>

</blueprint>
```

We drop this `route2.xml` file into the `deploy` folder of Karaf.

Now, we can see the following in the Karaf log:

```
2014-12-15 17:04:11,258 | INFO  | :///tmp/exchange | route2 | 70 -
org.apache.camel.camel-core - 2.12.4 | Exchange[ExchangePattern:
InOnly, BodyType: String, Body: Hello chapter5i]
```

```
2014-12-15 17:04:11,260 | INFO  | :///tmp/exchange | route2 | 70 -
org.apache.camel.camel-core - 2.12.4 | Exchange[ExchangePattern:
InOnly, BodyType: String, Body: Hello chapter5i]

2014-12-15 17:04:11,260 | INFO  | :///tmp/exchange | route2 | 70 -
org.apache.camel.camel-core - 2.12.4 | Exchange[ExchangePattern:
InOnly, BodyType: String, Body: Hello chapter5i]

2014-12-15 17:04:11,261 | INFO  | :///tmp/exchange | route2 | 70 -
org.apache.camel.camel-core - 2.12.4 | Exchange[ExchangePattern:
InOnly, BodyType: String, Body: Hello chapter5i]

2014-12-15 17:04:11,262 | INFO  | :///tmp/exchange | route2 | 70 -
org.apache.camel.camel-core - 2.12.4 | Exchange[ExchangePattern:
InOnly, BodyType: String, Body: Hello chapter5i]

2014-12-15 17:04:11,263 | INFO  | :///tmp/exchange | route2 | 70 -
org.apache.camel.camel-core - 2.12.4 | Exchange[ExchangePattern:
InOnly, BodyType: String, Body: Hello chapter5i]

2014-12-15 17:04:11,263 | INFO  | :///tmp/exchange | route2 | 70 -
org.apache.camel.camel-core - 2.12.4 | Exchange[ExchangePattern:
InOnly, BodyType: String, Body: Hello chapter5i]
```

So even if the second route is not deployed, the messages are not lost and stored on the filesystem. It's an implementation of the Guaranteed Delivery EIP.

Message Bus

The Message Bus EIP describes the architecture to plug and play applications that have to interact. This EIP gathers the messaging infrastructure, and the other layers required to implement routing.

So, basically, Camel itself is an implementation of the Message Bus EIP.

Message Construction EIPs

These EIPs are responsible for creating messages in response to other messages.

The Event Message EIP

The Event Message EIP describes how to use messaging to transmit events from one application to another.

Camel supports this EIP by the use of the Message Exchange Pattern in the exchange. When defined as `InOnly`, it means that we deal with a one way event message.

So, basically, the Event Message EIP means one directional messages.

The first endpoint of the route defines the expected Exchange pattern, but, at any point in the route, you can force the Exchange pattern to `InOnly` to make it act as an Event Message EIP.

For this, you have to use the `inOnly` notation:

```
<route>
    <from uri="direct:start"/>
    <inOnly uri="bean:myBean"/>
</route>
```

You can also use the `setExchangePattern` notation:

```
<route>
    <from uri="direct:start"/>
    <setExchangePattern pattern="InOnly"/>
    <to uri="bean:myBean"/>
</route>
```

It's also possible to define the pattern as an attribute of the endpoint:

```
<route>
    <from uri="direct:start"/>
    <to uri="bean:myBean" pattern="InOnly"/>
</route>
```

The Request Reply EIP

The Request Reply EIP is like the Event Message EIP, but this time, a response is expected from the target application.

As it does with Event Message, Camel supports this EIP using the Message Exchange pattern defined as `InOut`.

Again, the `from` endpoint defines the pattern that it expects. For instance, a CXF endpoint will define the pattern as `InOut` as it has to return something to the client.

As in the `InOnly` pattern, you can *force* the pattern to `InOut`, using the same notations.

The Correlation Identifier EIP

The Correlation Identifier EIP is useful when used with the Request Reply pattern. With this pattern, an identifier can be added to a message, which can be used to correlate the response message with the request message.

Camel supports this EIP by defining a dedicated header in the message or a property on the exchange. This header (or a property) is actually the Correlation Identifier.

Some other EIPs (that we will see later) leverage this header to correlate multiple messages all together. For instance, the Splitter EIP defines the Correlation Identifier as a property of the exchanges resulting from the split (for instance, to be able to aggregate the messages).

The Return Address EIP

The Return Address EIP describes how a target endpoint knows where it has to send a response. This EIP has to be used in combination with the Request Reply pattern, as we expect a response from the target endpoint.

Camel supports this EIP by populating a JMSReplyTo header in the message in the case of the JMS endpoints involved.

When working with the JMS component, this JMSReplyTo header is directly used and transported by the broker.

It's also possible to use the ReplyTo option on the JMS endpoint to populate the JMSReplyTo header on the fly:

```
<to uri="jms:queue:request?replyTo=response"/>
```

Message Routing

These EIPs are the core routing patterns. It's mostly where Camel provides specific syntax to handle routing.

The Content Based Router EIP

The Content Based Router EIP is a special case of the Message Router EIP.

As we've seen previously, the Message Router EIP is a generic routing EIP defining a conditional routing on the message.

The Content Based Router EIP is used in cases where the condition is based on the content of the body of the message itself. In the Message Router example, the condition was on the extension of the consumed files.

Here, to illustrate the Content Based Router EIP, we create an example that will route the files depending on an XPath predicate in the body of the message.

We create the following route.xml Blueprint description:

```xml
<?xml version="1.0" encoding="UTF-8"?>
<blueprint xmlns="http://www.osgi.org/xmlns/blueprint/v1.0.0">

  <camelContext xmlns="http://camel.apache.org/schema/blueprint">
      <route>
          <from uri="file:/tmp/in"/>
          <choice>
              <when>
                  <xpath>//address='France'</xpath>
                  <to uri="file:/tmp/out/france"/>
              </when>
              <when>
                  <xpath>//address='USA'</xpath>
                  <to uri="file:/tmp/out/usa"/>
              </when>
              <otherwise>
                  <to uri="file:/tmp/out/others"/>
              </otherwise>
          </choice>
      </route>
  </camelContext>

</blueprint>
```

The route consumes files from the /tmp/in folder. The message body contains the contents of the file. We use the XPath predicates to test the address element in the message, as follows:

*   If the address is France, the message is routed to the /tmp/out/france folder.

*   If the address is USA, the message is routed to the /tmp/out/usa folder.

*   If the address is not France or USA, the message is routed to the /tmp/out/others folder.

We start Karaf and install the `camel-blueprint` feature:

```
$ bin/karaf

karaf@root()> feature:repo-add camel 2.12.4

Adding feature url mvn:org.apache.camel.karaf/apache-
camel/2.12.4/xml/features

karaf@root()> feature:install camel-blueprint
```

We drop the `route.xml` into the Karaf `deploy` folder. In the `/tmp/in` folder, we create the `first.xml` file, containing:

```
<person>
<name>jbonofre</name>
<address>France</address>
</person>
```

We also drop the `second.xml` file, containing:

```
<person>
<name>Bob</name>
<address>USA</address>
</person>
```

We also drop the `third.xml` file, containing:

```
<person>
<name>Juan</name>
<address>Spain</address>
</person>
```

We can see that the files have been routed to different folders, as expected:

```
/tmp/out$ tree
.
├── france
│   └── first.xml
├── others
│   └── third.xml
└── usa
    └── second.xml
```

The Message Filter EIP

The Message Filter EIP describes how to select only the messages that we want to process.

We define a predicate to match and process the messages. If the messages don't match, their predicate will be ignored.

As in the Message Router EIP, we can use any language supported by Camel to write the predicate.

To illustrate the Message Filter EIP, we use the following `route.xml` Blueprint descriptor:

```xml
<?xml version="1.0" encoding="UTF-8"?>
<blueprint xmlns="http://www.osgi.org/xmlns/blueprint/v1.0.0">

  <camelContext xmlns="http://camel.apache.org/schema/blueprint">
      <route>
          <from uri="file:/tmp/in"/>
          <filter>
              <xpath>//name='jbonofre'</xpath>
              <to uri="direct:next"/>
          </filter>
      </route>
      <route>
          <from uri="direct:next"/>
          <convertBodyTo type="java.lang.String"/>
          <to uri="log:file"/>
      </route>
  </camelContext>

</blueprint>
```

The first route consumes the files from the `/tmp/in` folder. If the file contains the name element with `jbonofre`, the message is moved forward to the second route (thanks to the `direct` endpoint).

If the `XPath` predicate is not matched, the message is ignored.

We start Karaf and install the `camel-blueprint` feature:

```
$ bin/karaf
karaf@root()> feature:repo-add camel 2.12.4
```

```
Adding feature url mvn:org.apache.camel.karaf/apache-
camel/2.12.4/xml/features

karaf@root()> feature:install camel-blueprint
```

In the `/tmp/in` folder, we create the same three files as we did in the previous example.

The `first.xml` file, containing:

```
<person>
<name>jbonofre</name>
<address>France</address>
</person>
```

The `second.xml` file, containing:

```
<person>
<name>Bob</name>
<address>USA</address>
</person>
```

The `third.xml` file, containing:

```
<person>
<name>Juan</name>
<address>Spain</address>
</person>
```

In the Karaf `log` file, we can see:

```
2014-12-15 18:12:10,944 | INFO  | - file:///tmp/in | file | 70 -
org.apache.camel.camel-core - 2.12.4 | Exchange[ExchangePattern:
InOnly, BodyType: String, Body:

<person><name>jbonofre</name><address>France</address></person>]
```

This means that only the message from the `first.xml` file has been processed.

The Dynamic Router EIP

The Dynamic Router EIP describes how to dynamically route the message. When using the Message Router EIP, the different routing destinations and the conditions are statically defined at design time.

With the Dynamic Router EIP, the condition and the destinations are evaluated at runtime, and so, can be changed dynamically.

It's also possible to send the message to multiple destinations on one condition.

To illustrate this EIP, we create a route that uses a dynamic router. The dynamic router uses a bean to evaluate the condition and define the routing destinations.

We create a very simple Maven `pom.xml` file:

```xml
<?xml version="1.0" encoding="UTF-8"?>
<project xmlns="http://maven.apache.org/POM/4.0.0"
xmlns:xsi="http://www.w3.org/2001/XMLSchema-instance"
xsi:schemaLocation="http://maven.apache.org/POM/4.0.0
http://maven.apache.org/xsd/maven-4.0.0.xsd">

  <modelVersion>4.0.0</modelVersion>

  <groupId>com.packt.camel</groupId>
  <artifactId>chapter51</artifactId>
  <version>1.0-SNAPSHOT</version>
  <packaging>bundle</packaging>

  <build>
      <plugins>
          <plugin>
              <groupId>org.apache.felix</groupId>
              <artifactId>maven-bundle-plugin</artifactId>
              <version>2.3.7</version>
              <extensions>true</extensions>
              <configuration>
                  <instructions>
                      <Import-Package>*</Import-Package>
                  </instructions>
              </configuration>
          </plugin>
      </plugins>
  </build>

</project>
```

This Maven `pom.xml` file just packages the route and the bean as an OSGi bundle.

We create the `DynamicRouterBean` class:

```java
package com.packt.camel.chapter51;

import java.util.Random;

public class DynamicRouterBean {

  public String slip(String body) {
```

```
Random random = new Random();
int value = random.nextInt(1000);
if (value >= 500) {
    return "direct:large";
} else {
    return "direct:small";
}
}
}
```

This bean randomly and dynamically routes the message to two endpoints—if the generated random number is greater than 500, the message is routed to the direct:large endpoint, otherwise, the message is routed to the direct:small endpoint.

We now create the route using a Blueprint descriptor:

```xml
<?xml version="1.0" encoding="UTF-8"?>
<blueprint xmlns="http://www.osgi.org/xmlns/blueprint/v1.0.0">

    <bean id="dynamicRouterBean"
      class="com.packt.camel.chapter5l.DynamicRouterBean"/>

    <camelContext xmlns="http://camel.apache.org/schema/blueprint">
        <route>
            <from uri="timer:fire?period=5000"/>
            <setBody>
                <constant>Hello chapter5l</constant>
            </setBody>
            <dynamicRouter>
                <method ref="dynamicRouterBean" method="slip"/>
            </dynamicRouter>
        </route>
        <route>
            <from uri="direct:large"/>
            <to uri="log:large"/>
        </route>
        <route>
            <from uri="direct:small"/>
            <to uri="log:small"/>
        </route>
    </camelContext>

</blueprint>
```

This route uses the bean in the `dynamicRouter` notation. We create the two routes corresponding to the target endpoints of the dynamic router.

We build our OSGi bundle with:

```
$ mvn clean install
```

Our bundle is now ready to be deployed in Karaf.

We start Karaf and install the `camel-blueprint` feature:

```
$ bin/karaf
karaf@root()> feature:repo-add camel 2.12.4
Adding feature url mvn:org.apache.camel.karaf/apache-
camel/2.12.4/xml/features
karaf@root()> feature:install camel-blueprint
```

We deploy and start our bundle:

```
karaf@root()> bundle:install -s mvn:com.packt.camel/chapter51/1.0-
SNAPSHOT
Bundle ID: 73
```

In the Karaf `log` file, we can see:

```
2014-12-15 18:45:48,518 | INFO  | 1 - timer://fire | large | 70 -
org.apache.camel.camel-core - 2.12.4 | Exchange[ExchangePattern:
InOnly, BodyType: String, Body: Hello chapter51]

2014-12-15 18:45:48,518 | INFO  | 1 - timer://fire | small | 70 -
org.apache.camel.camel-core - 2.12.4 | Exchange[ExchangePattern:
InOnly, BodyType: String, Body: Hello chapter51]

2014-12-15 18:45:48,518 | INFO  | 1 - timer://fire | large | 70 -
org.apache.camel.camel-core - 2.12.4 | Exchange[ExchangePattern:
InOnly, BodyType: String, Body: Hello chapter51]

2014-12-15 18:45:48,519 | INFO  | 1 - timer://fire | small | 70 -
org.apache.camel.camel-core - 2.12.4 | Exchange[ExchangePattern:
InOnly, BodyType: String, Body: Hello chapter51]

2014-12-15 18:45:48,519 | INFO  | 1 - timer://fire | large | 70 -
org.apache.camel.camel-core - 2.12.4 | Exchange[ExchangePattern:
InOnly, BodyType: String, Body: Hello chapter51]

2014-12-15 18:45:48,519 | INFO  | 1 - timer://fire | large | 70 -
org.apache.camel.camel-core - 2.12.4 | Exchange[ExchangePattern:
InOnly, BodyType: String, Body: Hello chapter51]

2014-12-15 18:45:48,519 | INFO  | 1 - timer://fire | large | 70 -
org.apache.camel.camel-core - 2.12.4 | Exchange[ExchangePattern:
InOnly, BodyType: String, Body: Hello chapter51]
```

Multicast and Recipient List EIPs

The Recipient List EIP describes how to send the same message to multiple destinations.

We have two kinds of Recipient List:

- When the destinations are statically defined (at design time), we talk about the static Recipient List or multicast.
- When the destinations are dynamically defined (at runtime), we talk about the dynamic recipient list

The Multicast EIP

Let's start with a first example of the Multicast EIP (or a static recipient list).

We create the following `route.xml` Blueprint descriptor:

```xml
<?xml version="1.0" encoding="UTF-8"?>
<blueprint xmlns="http://www.osgi.org/xmlns/blueprint/v1.0.0">

  <camelContext xmlns="http://camel.apache.org/schema/blueprint">
      <route>
          <from uri="timer:first?period=5000"/>
          <setBody><constant>Hello chapter5m</constant></setBody>
          <multicast>
              <to uri="direct:france"/>
              <to uri="direct:usa"/>
              <to uri="direct:spain"/>
          </multicast>
      </route>
      <route>
          <from uri="direct:france"/>
          <to uri="log:france"/>
      </route>
      <route>
          <from uri="direct:usa"/>
          <to uri="log:usa"/>
      </route>
      <route>
          <from uri="direct:spain"/>
          <to uri="log:spain"/>
      </route>
  </camelContext>

</blueprint>
```

The first route creates a `Hello chapter5m` message every 5 seconds. This message is sent to three destinations, `france`, `usa`, and `spain`.

We start Karaf and install the `camel-blueprint` feature:

```
$ bin/karaf
karaf@root()> feature:repo-add camel 2.12.4
Adding feature url mvn:org.apache.camel.karaf/apache-
camel/2.12.4/xml/features
karaf@root()> feature:install camel-blueprint
```

We drop our `route.xml` file into the Karaf `deploy` folder.

In the Karaf `log` file, we can see:

```
2014-12-15 18:59:17,198 | INFO  |  - timer://first | france | 70 -
org.apache.camel.camel-core - 2.12.4 | Exchange[ExchangePattern:
InOnly, BodyType: String, Body: Hello chapter5m]
2014-12-15 18:59:17,199 | INFO  |  - timer://first | usa | 70 -
org.apache.camel.camel-core - 2.12.4 | Exchange[ExchangePattern:
InOnly, BodyType: String, Body: Hello chapter5m]
2014-12-15 18:59:17,200 | INFO  |  - timer://first | spain | 70 -
org.apache.camel.camel-core - 2.12.4 | Exchange[ExchangePattern:
InOnly, BodyType: String, Body: Hello chapter5m]
2014-12-15 18:59:22,180 | INFO  |  - timer://first | france | 70 -
org.apache.camel.camel-core - 2.12.4 | Exchange[ExchangePattern:
InOnly, BodyType: String, Body: Hello chapter5m]
2014-12-15 18:59:22,182 | INFO  |  - timer://first | usa | 70 -
org.apache.camel.camel-core - 2.12.4 | Exchange[ExchangePattern:
InOnly, BodyType: String, Body: Hello chapter5m]
2014-12-15 18:59:22,183 | INFO  |  - timer://first | spain | 70 -
org.apache.camel.camel-core - 2.12.4 | Exchange[ExchangePattern:
InOnly, BodyType: String, Body: Hello chapter5m]
```

We can see that each message has been sent to the three destinations.

The Recipient List EIP

To illustrate a dynamic recipient list, we create a route that uses a bean to dynamically define the target destinations.

We create a simple Maven `pom.xml` file:

```
<?xml version="1.0" encoding="UTF-8"?>
<project xmlns="http://maven.apache.org/POM/4.0.0"
xmlns:xsi="http://www.w3.org/2001/XMLSchema-instance"
xsi:schemaLocation="http://maven.apache.org/POM/4.0.0
http://maven.apache.org/xsd/maven-4.0.0.xsd">

  <modelVersion>4.0.0</modelVersion>

  <groupId>com.packt.camel</groupId>
  <artifactId>chapter5n</artifactId>
  <version>1.0-SNAPSHOT</version>
  <packaging>bundle</packaging>

  <build>
      <plugins>
          <plugin>
              <groupId>org.apache.felix</groupId>
              <artifactId>maven-bundle-plugin</artifactId>
              <version>2.3.7</version>
              <extensions>true</extensions>
              <configuration>
                  <instructions>
                      <Import-Package>*</Import-Package>
                  </instructions>
              </configuration>
          </plugin>
      </plugins>
  </build>

</project>
```

This Maven `pom.xml` file just packages our route and the bean as an OSGi bundle.

We create a simple `RouterBean` class that randomly changes the recipient list:

```
package com.packt.camel.chapter5n;

import java.util.Random;

public class RouterBean {

  public String populate(String body) {
      Random random = new Random();
```

```
        int value = random.nextInt(1000);
        if (value >= 500) {
            return "direct:one,direct:two,direct:three";
        } else {
            return "direct:one,direct:two";
        }
    }
}
```

If the random integer is greater than 500, the message is routed to the direct:one, direct:two, and direct:three endpoints. Otherwise, the message is just routed to the direct:one and direct:two endpoints.

Finally, we use this bean to populate a header in a route. This header is used by the recipient list:

```xml
<?xml version="1.0" encoding="UTF-8"?>
<blueprint xmlns="http://www.osgi.org/xmlns/blueprint/v1.0.0">

  <bean id="routerBean"
    class="com.packt.camel.chapter5n.RouterBean"/>

  <camelContext xmlns="http://camel.apache.org/schema/blueprint">
    <route>
        <from uri="timer:fire?period=5000"/>
        <setBody>
            <constant>Hello chapter5n</constant>
        </setBody>
        <setHeader headerName="recipientList">
            <method bean="routerBean" method="populate"/>
        </setHeader>
        <recipientList delimiter=",">
            <header>recipientList</header>
        </recipientList>
    </route>
    <route>
        <from uri="direct:one"/>
        <to uri="log:one"/>
    </route>
    <route>
        <from uri="direct:two"/>
        <to uri="log:two"/>
    </route>
    <route>
        <from uri="direct:three"/>
```

```
                <to uri="log:three"/>
        </route>
    </camelContext>

</blueprint>
```

We build our bundle:

```
$ mvn clean install
```

Our bundle is ready to be deployed in Karaf.

We start Karaf and install the `camel-blueprint` feature:

```
$ bin/karaf

karaf@root()> feature:repo-add camel 2.12.4

Adding feature url mvn:org.apache.camel.karaf/apache-
camel/2.12.4/xml/features

karaf@root()> feature:install camel-blueprint
```

We install our bundle:

```
karaf@root()> bundle:install -s mvn:com.packt.camel/chapter5n/1.0-
SNAPSHOT

Bundle ID: 73
```

In the Karaf `log` file, we can see:

```
2014-12-15 19:12:32,975 | INFO  | 1 - timer://fire | one | 70 -
org.apache.camel.camel-core - 2.12.4 | Exchange[ExchangePattern:
InOnly, BodyType: String, Body: Hello chapter5n]

2014-12-15 19:12:32,976 | INFO  | 1 - timer://fire | two | 70 -
org.apache.camel.camel-core - 2.12.4 | Exchange[ExchangePattern:
InOnly, BodyType: String, Body: Hello chapter5n]

2014-12-15 19:12:37,949 | INFO  | 1 - timer://fire | one | 70 -
org.apache.camel.camel-core - 2.12.4 | Exchange[ExchangePattern:
InOnly, BodyType: String, Body: Hello chapter5n]

2014-12-15 19:12:37,950 | INFO  | 1 - timer://fire | two | 70 -
org.apache.camel.camel-core - 2.12.4 | Exchange[ExchangePattern:
InOnly, BodyType: String, Body: Hello chapter5n]

2014-12-15 19:12:37,950 | INFO  | 1 - timer://fire | three | 70 -
org.apache.camel.camel-core - 2.12.4 | Exchange[ExchangePattern:
InOnly, BodyType: String, Body: Hello chapter5n]
```

We can see that the destinations dynamically change, depending on the result of the randomized integer.

The Splitter and Aggregator EIPs

These EIPs are responsible for splitting a big message into chunks, or aggregating small chunks in one whole message.

The Splitter EIP

The Splitter EIP describes how to split big messages into multiple chunks, processed individually.

Camel supports this EIP, allowing you to define the splitting logic using any supported language or a processor/bean.

To illustrate the Splitter EIP, we create the following `route.xml` Blueprint descriptor:

```xml
<?xml version="1.0" encoding="UTF-8"?>
<blueprint xmlns="http://www.osgi.org/xmlns/blueprint/v1.0.0">

  <camelContext xmlns="http://camel.apache.org/schema/blueprint">
      <route>
          <from uri="file:/tmp/in"/>
          <split>
              <xpath>//person</xpath>
              <to uri="log:chunk"/>
          </split>
      </route>
  </camelContext>

</blueprint>
```

This route consumes files from the `/tmp/in` folder, and splits the content using `XPath`.

We start Karaf and install the `camel-blueprint` feature:

```
$ bin/karaf
karaf@root()> feature:repo-add camel 2.12.4
karaf@root()> feature:install camel-blueprint
```

We drop the `route.xml` into the Karaf `deploy` folder.

In the `/tmp/in` folder, we create the following `persons.xml` file:

```xml
<persons>
   <person>
    <name>jbonofre</name>
```

```
    <address>France</address>
   </person>
   <person>
    <name>Bob</name>
    <address>USA</address>
   </person>
   <person>
    <name>Juan</name>
    <address>Spain</address>
   </person>
  </persons>
```

In the Karaf `log` file, we can see:

```
2014-12-15 19:30:35,624 | INFO  | - file:///tmp/in | chunk | 70 -
org.apache.camel.camel-core - 2.12.4 | Exchange[ExchangePattern:
InOnly, BodyType: org.apache.xerces.dom.DeferredElementNSImpl, Body:
<person> <name>jbonofre</name> <address>France</address> </person>]

2014-12-15 19:30:35,624 | INFO  | - file:///tmp/in | chunk | 70 -
org.apache.camel.camel-core - 2.12.4 | Exchange[ExchangePattern:
InOnly, BodyType: org.apache.xerces.dom.DeferredElementNSImpl, Body:
<person> <name>Bob</name> <address>USA</address>    </person>]

2014-12-15 19:30:35,625 | INFO  | - file:///tmp/in | chunk | 70 -
org.apache.camel.camel-core - 2.12.4 | Exchange[ExchangePattern:
InOnly, BodyType: org.apache.xerces.dom.DeferredElementNSImpl, Body:
<person>    <name>Juan</name>    <address>Spain</address> </person>]
```

We can see that the *big* file has been split into *small* messages.

 Camel supports multiple split strategies (using languages, tokens, custom beans, and so on).

Aggregator

The Aggregator EIP is the exact opposite of the Splitter EIP—we receive multiple *small* messages that we want to aggregate into one *big* message.

Camel supports this EIP. You have to provide two things to the aggregator:

- A bean implementing Camel `AggregationStrategy`, which defines the way you aggregate the new message with the previously aggregated message (the *message growing*)

- The aggregation completion, which defines when we consider the aggregation to be complete

You have different alternatives for the completion of the following task:

- The `completionTimeout` is an inactivity timeout. If no new exchanges come into the aggregator after this timeout, the aggregation is considered to be complete.

- The `completionInterval` considers the aggregation to be complete after a given amount of time.

- The `completionSize` is a static number of exchanges to aggregate.

- The `completionPredicate` is the most evolved. The aggregation is considered to be complete when the predicate is true.

To illustrate the Aggregator EIP, we create a route that aggregates a static number of messages.

We package the bean (used for the aggregation strategy) and the route definition as an OSGi bundle.

We create the following Maven `pom.xml`:

```xml
<?xml version="1.0" encoding="UTF-8"?>
<project xmlns="http://maven.apache.org/POM/4.0.0"
xmlns:xsi="http://www.w3.org/2001/XMLSchema-instance"
xsi:schemaLocation="http://maven.apache.org/POM/4.0.0
http://maven.apache.org/xsd/maven-4.0.0.xsd">

  <modelVersion>4.0.0</modelVersion>

  <groupId>com.packt.camel</groupId>
  <artifactId>chapter5p</artifactId>
  <version>1.0-SNAPSHOT</version>
  <packaging>bundle</packaging>

  <dependencies>
     <dependency>
         <groupId>org.apache.camel</groupId>
         <artifactId>camel-core</artifactId>
         <version>2.12.4</version>
     </dependency>
  </dependencies>

  <build>
     <plugins>
         <plugin>
             <groupId>org.apache.felix</groupId>
             <artifactId>maven-bundle-plugin</artifactId>
```

```
            <version>2.3.7</version>
            <extensions>true</extensions>
            <configuration>
                <instructions>
                    <Import-Package>*</Import-Package>
                </instructions>
            </configuration>
        </plugin>
    </plugins>
  </build>

</project>
```

We create the `StringAggregator` class, which implements an aggregation strategy appending strings:

```
package com.packt.camel.chapter5p;

import org.apache.camel.Exchange;
import org.apache.camel.processor.aggregate.AggregationStrategy;

public class StringAggregator implements AggregationStrategy {

    public Exchange aggregate(Exchange oldExchange, Exchange
                              newExchange) {
        if (oldExchange == null) {
            return newExchange;
        }
        String oldBody = oldExchange.getIn().getBody(String.class);
        String newBody = newExchange.getIn().getBody(String.class);
        oldExchange.getIn().setBody(oldBody + "+" + newBody);
        return oldExchange;
    }

}
```

We create the route using the Blueprint DSL with an aggregator with our `StringAggregator` and a `completionSize` class:

```
<?xml version="1.0" encoding="UTF-8"?>
<blueprint xmlns="http://www.osgi.org/xmlns/blueprint/v1.0.0">

   <bean id="aggregator" class="com.packt.camel.chapter5p.
StringAggregator"/>

   <camelContext xmlns="http://camel.apache.org/schema/blueprint">
```

```
        <route>
            <from uri="timer:fire?period=5000"/>
            <setBody>
                <constant>Hello chapter5p</constant>
            </setBody>
            <setHeader headerName="id">
                <constant>same</constant>
            </setHeader>
            <aggregate strategyRef="aggregator" completionSize="5">
                <correlationExpression>
                    <simple>header.id</simple>
                </correlationExpression>
                <to uri="log:aggregated"/>
            </aggregate>
        </route>
    </camelContext>

</blueprint>
```

The messages correlation (to identify that we are in the same aggregation unit) is defined using the header ID. This route aggregates five messages together.

We build our OSGi bundle:

```
$ mvn clean install
```

Our bundle is ready to be deployed in Karaf.

We start Karaf and install the `camel-blueprint` feature:

```
$ bin/karaf
karaf@root()> feature:repo-add camel 2.12.4
Adding feature url mvn:org.apache.camel.karaf/apache-
camel/2.12.4/xml/features
karaf@root()> feature:install camel-blueprint
```

We install and start our bundle:

```
karaf@root()> bundle:install -s mvn:com.packt.camel/chapter5p/1.0-
SNAPSHOT
Bundle ID: 73
```

In the Karaf `log` file, we can see:

```
2014-12-15 21:07:22,386 | INFO  | 1 - timer://fire | aggregated | 70
- org.apache.camel.camel-core - 2.12.4 | Exchange[ExchangePattern:
InOnly, BodyType: String, Body: Hello chapter5p+Hello chapter5p+Hello
chapter5p+Hello chapter5p+Hello chapter5p]
```

```
2014-12-15 21:07:47,380 | INFO | 1 - timer://fire | aggregated | 70
- org.apache.camel.camel-core - 2.12.4 | Exchange[ExchangePattern:
InOnly, BodyType: String, Body: Hello chapter5p+Hello chapter5p+Hello
chapter5p+Hello chapter5p+Hello chapter5p]
```

We can see that our route aggregated 5 `Hello chapter5p` messages.

The Resequencer EIP

The Resequencer EIP describes how to sort the processing of the messages. It uses a comparator to define the sequence of the messages.

Camel uses an expression to create the comparator. It means that the comparator can use the body of the message, a header, and so on. You define the expression in the Camel resequencer notation.

To illustrate the Resequencer EIP, we use the following `route.xml` Blueprint descriptor:

```
<?xml version="1.0" encoding="UTF-8"?>
<blueprint xmlns="http://www.osgi.org/xmlns/blueprint/v1.0.0">

    <camelContext xmlns="http://camel.apache.org/schema/blueprint">
        <route>
            <from uri="timer:first?period=2000"/>
            <setBody><constant>one</constant></setBody>
            <to uri="direct:resequencer"/>
        </route>
        <route>
            <from uri="timer:second?period=2000"/>
            <setBody><constant>two</constant></setBody>
            <to uri="direct:resequencer"/>
        </route>
        <route>
            <from uri="direct:resequencer"/>
            <resequence>
                <simple>body</simple>
                <to uri="log:requencer"/>
            </resequence>
        </route>
    </camelContext>

</blueprint>
```

Two routes generate a message every 2 seconds. Both routes send the message to the resequencer route. The resequencer uses a string comparator on the body of the messages, to guarantee the same processing order, one first, two after.

We start Karaf and install the `camel-blueprint` feature:

```
$ bin/karaf
karaf@root()> feature:repo-add camel 2.12.4
Adding feature url mvn:org.apache.camel.karaf/apache-camel/2.12.4/xml/
features
karaf@root()> feature:install camel-blueprint
```

We drop the `route.xml` file into the Karaf `deploy` folder.

In the Karaf `log` file, we can see:

```
2014-12-15 21:22:16,769 | INFO  | 0 - Batch Sender | requencer | 70 -
org.apache.camel.camel-core - 2.12.4 | Exchange[ExchangePattern:
InOnly, BodyType: String, Body: one]
2014-12-15 21:22:16,770 | INFO  | 0 - Batch Sender | requencer | 70 -
org.apache.camel.camel-core - 2.12.4 | Exchange[ExchangePattern:
InOnly, BodyType: String, Body: two]
2014-12-15 21:22:18,746 | INFO  | 0 - Batch Sender | requencer | 70 -
org.apache.camel.camel-core - 2.12.4 | Exchange[ExchangePattern:
InOnly, BodyType: String, Body: one]
2014-12-15 21:22:18,747 | INFO  | 0 - Batch Sender | requencer | 70 -
org.apache.camel.camel-core - 2.12.4 | Exchange[ExchangePattern:
InOnly, BodyType: String, Body: two]
```

We can see that the messages are always processed in the same sequence, one first, two after.

The Composed Message Processor EIP

The Composed Message Processor EIP is a combination of the Splitter EIP and the Aggregator EIP. The purpose is:

- To split a big message into chunk messages
- To process each chunk independently
- To reaggregate each chunk response as a big message again

Camel supports this EIP in two ways:

- Using a pure combination of the Splitter and Aggregator EIPs
- Using only Splitter

The later is the easiest to use. It allows you to define the aggregation strategy directly on the splitter. The aggregation completion is defined by the Splitter as he knows the number of chunks he has created.

We illustrate the splitter-based Composed Message Processor EIP with an example that splits a `persons.xml` file with XPath, processes each person individually, and reaggregates the resulting message as a big one.

We create the following Maven `pom.xml` file:

```
<?xml version="1.0" encoding="UTF-8"?>
<project xmlns="http://maven.apache.org/POM/4.0.0"
xmlns:xsi="http://www.w3.org/2001/XMLSchema-instance"
xsi:schemaLocation="http://maven.apache.org/POM/4.0.0
http://maven.apache.org/xsd/maven-4.0.0.xsd">

  <modelVersion>4.0.0</modelVersion>

  <groupId>com.packt.camel</groupId>
  <artifactId>chapter5r</artifactId>
  <version>1.0-SNAPSHOT</version>
  <packaging>bundle</packaging>

  <dependencies>
      <dependency>
          <groupId>org.apache.camel</groupId>
          <artifactId>camel-core</artifactId>
          <version>2.12.4</version>
      </dependency>
  </dependencies>

  <build>
      <plugins>
          <plugin>
              <groupId>org.apache.felix</groupId>
              <artifactId>maven-bundle-plugin</artifactId>
              <version>2.3.7</version>
              <extensions>true</extensions>
              <configuration>
                  <instructions>
                      <Import-Package>*</Import-Package>
                  </instructions>
              </configuration>
          </plugin>
```

```
      </plugins>
   </build>

</project>
```

We create a custom aggregation strategy, `MyAggregator`, that works directly using the message string:

```
package com.packt.camel.chapter5r;

import org.apache.camel.Exchange;
import org.apache.camel.processor.aggregate.AggregationStrategy;

public class MyAggregator implements AggregationStrategy {

  public Exchange aggregate(Exchange oldExchange, Exchange
                            newExchange) {

      if (oldExchange == null) {
          return newExchange;
      }

      String persons = oldExchange.getIn().getBody(String.class);
      String newPerson =
      newExchange.getIn().getBody(String.class);

      // put orders together separating by semi colon
      persons = persons + newPerson;
      oldExchange.getIn().setBody(persons);

      return oldExchange;
  }

}
```

We create a route using the Blueprint DSL:

```
<?xml version="1.0" encoding="UTF-8"?>
<blueprint xmlns="http://www.osgi.org/xmlns/blueprint/v1.0.0">

  <bean id="aggregator" class="com.packt.camel.chapter5r.
MyAggregator"/>

  <camelContext xmlns="http://camel.apache.org/schema/blueprint">
     <route>
```

```
        <from uri="file:/tmp/in"/>
        <split strategyRef="aggregator">
            <xpath>//person</xpath>
            <to uri="log:person"/>
        </split>
        <to uri="log:persons"/>
    </route>
  </camelContext>

</blueprint>
```

This route consumes files from the /tmp/in folder, splits the messages using an XPath expression, and reaggregates after using the MyAggregator strategy.

We can now compile our bundle:

$ mvn clean install

We start Karaf and install the camel-blueprint feature:

```
$ bin/karaf
karaf@root()> feature:repo-add camel 2.12.4
Adding feature url mvn:org.apache.camel.karaf/apache-camel/2.12.4/xml/features
karaf@root()> feature:install camel-blueprint
```

We install and start our bundle:

karaf@root()> bundle:install -s mvn:com.packt.camel/chapter5r/1.0-SNAPSHOT

Bundle ID: 73

In the Karaf log file, we can see:

**2014-12-15 21:42:38,803 | INFO | - file:///tmp/in | person | 70 -
org.apache.camel.camel-core - 2.12.4 | Exchange[ExchangePattern:
InOnly, BodyType: org.apache.xerces.dom.DeferredElementNSImpl, Body:
<person><name>jbonofre</name><address>France</address></person>]**

**2014-12-15 21:42:38,804 | INFO | - file:///tmp/in | person | 70 -
org.apache.camel.camel-core - 2.12.4 | Exchange[ExchangePattern:
InOnly, BodyType: org.apache.xerces.dom.DeferredElementNSImpl, Body:
<person><name>Bob</name><address>USA</address></person>]**

**2014-12-15 21:42:38,806 | INFO | - file:///tmp/in | person | 70 -
org.apache.camel.camel-core - 2.12.4 | Exchange[ExchangePattern:
InOnly, BodyType: org.apache.xerces.dom.DeferredElementNSImpl, Body:
<person><name>Juan</name><address>Spain</address></person>]**

```
2014-12-15 21:42:38,806 | INFO  | - file:///tmp/in | persons | 70 -
org.apache.camel.camel-core - 2.12.4 | Exchange[ExchangePattern:
InOnly, BodyType: String, Body:
<person><name>jbonofre</name><address>France</address></person><perso
n><name>Bob</name><address>USA</address></person><person><name>Juan</
name><address>Spain</address></person>]
```

We can see that the splitter isolated each person that has been processed individually. After the split, the messages have been reaggregated again, as we can see in the latest `log` message.

The Scatter-Gather EIP

The Scatter-Gather EIP is similar to the Composed Message Processor EIP, but instead of splitting and aggregating, we first use a recipient list (static or dynamic) and an aggregator with the response coming from the different recipients.

Camel supports this EIP with the combination of recipient list/multicast and aggregate.

The Routing Slip EIP

The Routing Slip EIP describes how to dynamically define the processing steps of a message.

In a Camel route, the routing steps are statically defined; it's the route itself. However, you can use the `routingSlip` notation to define the next steps of the routing at runtime.

It's exactly like a dynamic recipient list, but the processing is not in parallel, it's in sequence.

To illustrate this EIP, we create a route that uses a bean to position a header containing the next processing steps.

We create the following Maven `pom.xml` file:

```xml
<?xml version="1.0" encoding="UTF-8"?>
<project xmlns="http://maven.apache.org/POM/4.0.0"
xmlns:xsi="http://www.w3.org/2001/XMLSchema-instance"
xsi:schemaLocation="http://maven.apache.org/POM/4.0.0
http://maven.apache.org/xsd/maven-4.0.0.xsd">

  <modelVersion>4.0.0</modelVersion>

  <groupId>com.packt.camel</groupId>
```

```
<artifactId>chapter5s</artifactId>
<version>1.0-SNAPSHOT</version>
<packaging>bundle</packaging>

<build>
    <plugins>
        <plugin>
            <groupId>org.apache.felix</groupId>
            <artifactId>maven-bundle-plugin</artifactId>
            <version>2.3.7</version>
            <extensions>true</extensions>
            <configuration>
                <instructions>
                    <Import-Package>*</Import-Package>
                </instructions>
            </configuration>
        </plugin>
    </plugins>
</build>

</project>
```

We create the following `RoutingSlipBean` class, which randomly defines the next steps of the routing:

```
package com.packt.camel.chapter5s;

import java.util.Random;

public class RoutingSlipBean {

  public String nextSteps(String body) {
      Random random = new Random();
      int value = random.nextInt(1000);
      if (value >= 500) {
          return "direct:one,direct:two";
      } else {
          return "direct:one";
      }
  }

}
```

We use this bean in a Camel route written using the Blueprint DSL to define a slip header. This header is used by routingslip:

```xml
<?xml version="1.0" encoding="UTF-8"?>
<blueprint xmlns="http://www.osgi.org/xmlns/blueprint/v1.0.0">

  <bean id="routingSlipBean"
    class="com.packt.camel.chapter5s.RoutingSlipBean"/>

  <camelContext xmlns="http://camel.apache.org/schema/blueprint">
      <route>
          <from uri="timer:fire?period=5000"/>
          <setBody>
              <constant>Hello chapter5s</constant>
          </setBody>
          <setHeader headerName="slip">
              <method bean="routingSlipBean" method="nextSteps"/>
          </setHeader>
          <routingSlip uriDelimiter=",">
              <header>slip</header>
          </routingSlip>
      </route>
      <route>
          <from uri="direct:one"/>
          <to uri="log:one"/>
      </route>
      <route>
          <from uri="direct:two"/>
          <to uri="log:two"/>
      </route>
  </camelContext>

</blueprint>
```

We now build our OSGi bundle:

```
$ mvn clean install
```

Our bundle is ready to be deployed in Karaf.

We start Karaf and install the camel-blueprint feature:

```
$ bin/karaf
karaf@root()> feature:repo-add camel 2.12.4
Adding feature url mvn:org.apache.camel.karaf/apache-camel/2.12.4/xml/features
karaf@root()> feature:install camel-blueprint
```

We install and start our bundle:

```
karaf@root()> bundle:install -s mvn:com.packt.camel/chapter5s/1.0-
SNAPSHOT
Bundle ID: 73
```

In the Karaf `log` file, we can see:

```
2014-12-15 22:02:19,110 | INFO  | 1 - timer://fire | one | 70 -
org.apache.camel.camel-core - 2.12.4 | Exchange[ExchangePattern:
InOnly, BodyType: String, Body: Hello chapter5s]
2014-12-15 22:02:19,111 | INFO  | 1 - timer://fire | two | 70 -
org.apache.camel.camel-core - 2.12.4 | Exchange[ExchangePattern:
InOnly, BodyType: String, Body: Hello chapter5s]
2014-12-15 22:02:24,090 | INFO  | 1 - timer://fire | one | 70 -
org.apache.camel.camel-core - 2.12.4 | Exchange[ExchangePattern:
InOnly, BodyType: String, Body: Hello chapter5s]
2014-12-15 22:02:29,090 | INFO  | 1 - timer://fire | one | 70 -
org.apache.camel.camel-core - 2.12.4 | Exchange[ExchangePattern:
InOnly, BodyType: String, Body: Hello chapter5s]
2014-12-15 22:02:29,091 | INFO  | 1 - timer://fire | two | 70 -
org.apache.camel.camel-core - 2.12.4 | Exchange[ExchangePattern:
InOnly, BodyType: String, Body: Hello chapter5s]
2014-12-15 22:02:34,090 | INFO  | 1 - timer://fire | one | 70 -
org.apache.camel.camel-core - 2.12.4 | Exchange[ExchangePattern:
InOnly, BodyType: String, Body: Hello chapter5s]
2014-12-15 22:02:39,091 | INFO  | 1 - timer://fire | one | 70 -
org.apache.camel.camel-core - 2.12.4 | Exchange[ExchangePattern:
InOnly, BodyType: String, Body: Hello chapter5s]
```

We can see (with the timestamps) that, sometimes, both one and two steps/routes are called, and sometimes only one is called.

The Throttler and Sampling EIPs

These EIPs provide support of messaging Quality of Service (QoS). This allows you to implement some Service Level Agreement (SLA), limiting the threshold on some endpoints.

The Throttler EIP

The Throttler EIP describes how to limit the number of messages reaching an endpoint, to avoid it. This allows you to guarantee SLA on routes, parts of routes, and applications.

Camel supports this EIP by providing the `throttle` notation. On the Throttle, you define a given period, and the maximum number of messages (or requests) allowed in the period. This number of messages can be static, or dynamic (using a header for instance).

To illustrate the Throttler EIP, we create the following `route.xml` Blueprint descriptor:

```xml
<?xml version="1.0" encoding="UTF-8"?>
<blueprint xmlns="http://www.osgi.org/xmlns/blueprint/v1.0.0">

    <camelContext xmlns="http://camel.apache.org/schema/blueprint">
        <route>
            <from uri="timer:first?period=500"/>
            <setBody><constant>Hello chapter5t</constant></setBody>
            <throttle timePeriodMillis="2000">
                <constant>1</constant>
                <to uri="direct:sla"/>
            </throttle>
        </route>
        <route>
            <from uri="direct:sla"/>
            <to uri="log:sla"/>
        </route>
    </camelContext>

</blueprint>
```

We start Karaf and install the `camel-blueprint` feature:

```
$ bin/karaf
karaf@root()> feature:repo-add camel 2.12.4
Adding feature url mvn:org.apache.camel.karaf/apache-
camel/2.12.4/xml/features
karaf@root()> feature:install camel-blueprint
```

We drop the `route.xml` into the Karaf `deploy` folder.

In the Karaf `log` file, we can see:

```
2014-12-16 07:05:03,106 | INFO  |  - timer://first | sla | 70 -
org.apache.camel.camel-core - 2.12.4 | Exchange[ExchangePattern:
InOnly, BodyType: String, Body: Hello chapter5t]
2014-12-16 07:05:05,105 | INFO  |  - timer://first | sla | 70 -
org.apache.camel.camel-core - 2.12.4 | Exchange[ExchangePattern:
InOnly, BodyType: String, Body: Hello chapter5t]
```

```
2014-12-16 07:05:07,105 | INFO  |  - timer://first | sla | 70 -
org.apache.camel.camel-core - 2.12.4 | Exchange[ExchangePattern:
InOnly, BodyType: String, Body: Hello chapter5t]

2014-12-16 07:05:09,105 | INFO  |  - timer://first | sla | 70 -
org.apache.camel.camel-core - 2.12.4 | Exchange[ExchangePattern:
InOnly, BodyType: String, Body: Hello chapter5t]

2014-12-16 07:05:11,104 | INFO  |  - timer://first | sla | 70 -
org.apache.camel.camel-core - 2.12.4 | Exchange[ExchangePattern:
InOnly, BodyType: String, Body: Hello chapter5t]
```

We can note the timestamp where we have only one message every two seconds, whereas the timer creates a message every 0.5 seconds; we have here an illustration of the Throttler EIP.

The Sampling EIP

The Sampling EIP is related to the Throttler EIP. The purpose is to take a message sample periodically:

- Every given number of messages
- Every given time

All the *other* traffic is ignored.

Camel supports this EIP via the usage of the `sample` notation. The sample notation supports the `messageFrequency` or `samplePeriod` properties.

To illustrate the Sampling EIP, we create the following `route.xml` blueprint XML descriptor:

```
<?xml version="1.0" encoding="UTF-8"?>
<blueprint xmlns="http://www.osgi.org/xmlns/blueprint/v1.0.0">

  <camelContext xmlns="http://camel.apache.org/schema/blueprint">
    <route>
      <from uri="timer:first?period=500"/>
      <setBody><constant>Hello chapter5u</constant></setBody>
      <to uri="log:regular"/>
      <sample messageFrequency="5">
        <to uri="direct:frequency"/>
      </sample>
    </route>
    <route>
      <from uri="direct:frequency"/>
```

```
        <to uri="log:frequency"/>
    </route>
  </camelContext>

</blueprint>
```

The first route creates a message every 0.5 seconds. We log with the `regular` log. We use a `sample` notation to send the fifth message to the frequency route (so every five messages, we send the sample).

We start Karaf and install the `camel-blueprint` feature:

```
karaf@root()> feature:repo-add camel 2.12.4

Adding feature url mvn:org.apache.camel.karaf/apache-
camel/2.12.4/xml/features

karaf@root()> feature:install camel-blueprint
```

We drop our `route.xml` file into the Karaf `deploy` folder.

In the Karaf `log` file, we can see:

```
2014-12-16 14:57:59,342 | INFO  | - timer://first | regular | 70 -
org.apache.camel.camel-core - 2.12.4 | Exchange[ExchangePattern:
InOnly, BodyType: String, Body: Hello chapter5u]

2014-12-16 14:57:59,824 | INFO  | - timer://first | regular | 70 -
org.apache.camel.camel-core - 2.12.4 | Exchange[ExchangePattern:
InOnly, BodyType: String, Body: Hello chapter5u]

2014-12-16 14:58:00,324 | INFO  | - timer://first | regular | 70 - org.
apache.camel.camel-core - 2.12.4 | Exchange[ExchangePattern:
InOnly, BodyType: String, Body: Hello chapter5u]

2014-12-16 14:58:00,824 | INFO  | - timer://first | regular | 70 -
org.apache.camel.camel-core - 2.12.4 | Exchange[ExchangePattern:
InOnly, BodyType: String, Body: Hello chapter5u]

2014-12-16 14:58:01,324 | INFO  | - timer://first | regular | 70 -
org.apache.camel.camel-core - 2.12.4 | Exchange[ExchangePattern:
InOnly, BodyType: String, Body: Hello chapter5u]

2014-12-16 14:58:01,325 | INFO  | - timer://first | frequency | 70 -
org.apache.camel.camel-core - 2.12.4 | Exchange[ExchangePattern:
InOnly, BodyType: String, Body: Hello chapter5u]

2014-12-16 14:58:01,824 | INFO  | - timer://first | regular | 70 -
org.apache.camel.camel-core - 2.12.4 | Exchange[ExchangePattern: InOnly,
BodyType: String, Body: Hello chapter5u]

2014-12-16 14:58:02,324 | INFO  | - timer://first | regular | 70 -
org.apache.camel.camel-core - 2.12.4 | Exchange[ExchangePattern:
InOnly, BodyType: String, Body: Hello chapter5u]
```

```
2014-12-16 14:58:02,825 | INFO  | - timer://first | regular | 70 -
org.apache.camel.camel-core - 2.12.4 | Exchange[ExchangePattern:
InOnly, BodyType: String, Body: Hello chapter5u]

2014-12-16 14:58:03,325 | INFO  | - timer://first | regular | 70 -
org.apache.camel.camel-core - 2.12.4 | Exchange[ExchangePattern: InOnly,
BodyType: String, Body: Hello chapter5u]

2014-12-16 14:58:03,825 | INFO  | - timer://first | regular | 70 -
org.apache.camel.camel-core - 2.12.4 | Exchange[ExchangePattern:
InOnly, BodyType: String, Body: Hello chapter5u]

2014-12-16 14:58:03,826 | INFO  | - timer://first | frequency | 70 -
org.apache.camel.camel-core - 2.12.4 | Exchange[ExchangePattern:
InOnly, BodyType: String, Body: Hello chapter5u]
```

So, we can see that the frequency route gets a `sample` notation for every five messages of regular load.

The Delayer EIP

The Delayer EIP allows you to add some kind of pause in the delivery of a message. It's like a sleep in the routing.

Camel supports this EIP using the `delay` notation. The delay notation accepts an expression to get the pause time. You can use any language supported by Camel for this expression.

We used this EIP in the `chapter5g` and `chapter5h` examples.

In these examples, we used a constant to define the delay time. It's also possible to use an expression returning the delay time. As always, the expression can be written using any language supported by Camel.

To illustrate the Delayer EIP with a dynamic delay time, we create a route that uses a bean to define the delay time (randomly).

We create the following Maven `pom.xml` file:

```xml
<?xml version="1.0" encoding="UTF-8"?>
<project xmlns="http://maven.apache.org/POM/4.0.0"
xmlns:xsi="http://www.w3.org/2001/XMLSchema-instance"
xsi:schemaLocation="http://maven.apache.org/POM/4.0.0
http://maven.apache.org/xsd/maven-4.0.0.xsd">

  <modelVersion>4.0.0</modelVersion>

  <groupId>com.packt.camel</groupId>
```

```
            <artifactId>chapter5v</artifactId>
            <version>1.0-SNAPSHOT</version>
            <packaging>bundle</packaging>

        <build>
            <plugins>
                <plugin>
                    <groupId>org.apache.felix</groupId>
                    <artifactId>maven-bundle-plugin</artifactId>
                    <version>2.3.7</version>
                    <extensions>true</extensions>
                    <configuration>
                        <instructions>
                            <Import-Package>*</Import-Package>
                        </instructions>
                    </configuration>
                </plugin>
            </plugins>
        </build>

    </project>
```

This Maven `pom.xml` file is very simple, just packaging the Blueprint XML definition of the route and the bean as an OSGi bundle.

We create a simple bean that randomly creates the delay time:

```
package com.packt.camel.chapter5v;

import java.util.Random;

public class DelayBean {

  public int delay() {
      Random random = new Random();
      return random.nextInt(10000);
  }

}
```

We create a route using the blueprint DSL:

```
<?xml version="1.0" encoding="UTF-8"?>
<blueprint xmlns="http://www.osgi.org/xmlns/blueprint/v1.0.0">

  <bean id="delayBean"
    class="com.packt.camel.chapter5v.DelayBean"/>

  <camelContext xmlns="http://camel.apache.org/schema/blueprint">
      <route>
          <from uri="timer:fire?period=1000"/>
          <setBody>
              <constant>Hello chapter5v</constant>
          </setBody>
          <delay>
              <method ref="delayBean" method="delay"/>
          </delay>
          <to uri="log:delay"/>
      </route>
  </camelContext>

</blueprint>
```

This route creates a message every second with a timer, and uses the bean in the `delay` notation.

We build our OSGi bundle:

```
$ mvn clean install
```

Our OSGi bundle is ready to be deployed in Karaf.

We start Karaf and install the `camel-blueprint` feature:

```
$ bin/karaf

karaf@root()> feature:repo-add camel 2.12.4

Adding feature url mvn:org.apache.camel.karaf/apache-camel/2.12.4/xml/
features

karaf@root()> feature:install camel-blueprint
```

We deploy our OSGi bundle in Karaf:

```
karaf@root()> bundle:install -s mvn:com.packt.camel/chapter5v/1.0-
SNAPSHOT

Bundle ID: 73
```

If we take a look in the Karaf `log` file, we can see:

```
2014-12-16 17:23:57,477 | INFO  | 1 - timer://fire | delay | 70 -
org.apache.camel.camel-core - 2.12.4 | Exchange[ExchangePattern:
InOnly, BodyType: String, Body: Hello chapter5v]

2014-12-16 17:23:58,914 | INFO  | 1 - timer://fire | delay | 70 -
org.apache.camel.camel-core - 2.12.4 | Exchange[ExchangePattern:
InOnly, BodyType: String, Body: Hello chapter5v]

2014-12-16 17:24:05,976 | INFO  | 1 - timer://fire | delay | 70 -
org.apache.camel.camel-core - 2.12.4 | Exchange[ExchangePattern:
InOnly, BodyType: String, Body: Hello chapter5v]

2014-12-16 17:24:14,083 | INFO  | 1 - timer://fire | delay | 70 -
org.apache.camel.camel-core - 2.12.4 | Exchange[ExchangePattern:
InOnly, BodyType: String, Body: Hello chapter5v]

2014-12-16 17:24:20,893 | INFO  | 1 - timer://fire | delay | 70 -
org.apache.camel.camel-core - 2.12.4 | Exchange[ExchangePattern:
InOnly, BodyType: String, Body: Hello chapter5v]

2014-12-16 17:24:30,350 | INFO  | 1 - timer://fire | delay | 70 -
org.apache.camel.camel-core - 2.12.4 | Exchange[ExchangePattern:
InOnly, BodyType: String, Body: Hello chapter5v]
```

We can note that the message is delivered randomly (see the timestamp), showing the Delayer EIP in action.

The Load Balancer EIP

The Load Balancer EIP dispatches the load of messages to different endpoints.

Camel supports this EIP with the `loadBalance` notation, which also supports different balancing policies such as:

- The round-robin policy uses a kind of *circle* between the different endpoints
- The random policy picks up one endpoint randomly
- The sticky policy uses an expression to select the target endpoint
- The topic policy sends the message to all the endpoints (like a JMS topic)
- The failover policy forwards the message to the next endpoint if the first target failed
- The weighted round-robin policy is like the round-robin policy, but you can give a ratio to the different endpoints to use them on high priority
- The weighted random policy is like the random policy, but you can give a ratio to the different endpoints to use them on high priority
- The custom policy allows you to implement your own load balancing policy

To illustrate the Load Balancer EIP, we use the following `route.xml` file:

```xml
<?xml version="1.0" encoding="UTF-8"?>
<blueprint xmlns="http://www.osgi.org/xmlns/blueprint/v1.0.0">

  <camelContext xmlns="http://camel.apache.org/schema/blueprint">
    <route>
      <from uri="timer:first?period=1000"/>
      <setBody><constant>Hello chapter5w</constant></setBody>
      <loadBalance>
        <roundRobin/>
        <to uri="direct:one"/>
        <to uri="direct:two"/>
        <to uri="direct:three"/>
      </loadBalance>
    </route>
    <route>
      <from uri="direct:one"/>
      <to uri="log:one"/>
    </route>
    <route>
      <from uri="direct:two"/>
      <to uri="log:two"/>
    </route>
    <route>
      <from uri="direct:three"/>
      <to uri="log:three"/>
    </route>
  </camelContext>

</blueprint>
```

The first route creates a message every second. The message is load balanced with the round-robin policy to the three endpoints: `direct:one`, `direct:two`, and `direct:three`.

We start Karaf and install the `camel-blueprint` feature:

```
$ bin/karaf

karaf@root()> feature:repo-add camel 2.12.4

Adding feature url mvn:org.apache.camel.karaf/apache-
camel/2.12.4/xml/features

karaf@root()> feature:install camel-blueprint
```

We drop the `route.xml` file into the Karaf `deploy` folder. In the Karaf `log` file, we can see:

```
2014-12-16 17:58:33,370 | INFO  |   - timer://first | one | 70 -
org.apache.camel.camel-core - 2.12.4 | Exchange[ExchangePattern:
InOnly, BodyType: String, Body: Hello chapter5w]
2014-12-16 17:58:34,356 | INFO  |   - timer://first | two | 70 -
org.apache.camel.camel-core - 2.12.4 | Exchange[ExchangePattern:
InOnly, BodyType: String, Body: Hello chapter5w]
2014-12-16 17:58:35,355 | INFO  |   - timer://first | three | 70 -
org.apache.camel.camel-core - 2.12.4 | Exchange[ExchangePattern:
InOnly, BodyType: String, Body: Hello chapter5w]
2014-12-16 17:58:36,355 | INFO  |   - timer://first | one | 70 -
org.apache.camel.camel-core - 2.12.4 | Exchange[ExchangePattern:
InOnly, BodyType: String, Body: Hello chapter5w]
2014-12-16 17:58:37,355 | INFO  |   - timer://first | two | 70 -
org.apache.camel.camel-core - 2.12.4 | Exchange[ExchangePattern:
InOnly, BodyType: String, Body: Hello chapter5w]
2014-12-16 17:58:38,355 | INFO  |   - timer://first | three | 70 -
org.apache.camel.camel-core - 2.12.4 | Exchange[ExchangePattern:
InOnly, BodyType: String, Body: Hello chapter5w]
2014-12-16 17:58:39,355 | INFO  |   - timer://first | one | 70 -
org.apache.camel.camel-core - 2.12.4 | Exchange[ExchangePattern:
InOnly, BodyType: String, Body: Hello chapter5w]
2014-12-16 17:58:40,356 | INFO  |   - timer://first | two | 70 -
org.apache.camel.camel-core - 2.12.4 | Exchange[ExchangePattern:
InOnly, BodyType: String, Body: Hello chapter5w]
```

Here, we note that each message is load balanced to the three endpoints in a round-robin manner.

The Loop EIP

The Loop EIP describes how to iterate a message on the same endpoint multiple times.

Camel supports this EIP using the `loop` notation. The number of iterations can be a constant, or the result of an expression (using any language supported by Camel).

To illustrate the Loop EIP, we create the following `route.xml` blueprint descriptor:

```xml
<?xml version="1.0" encoding="UTF-8"?>
<blueprint xmlns="http://www.osgi.org/xmlns/blueprint/v1.0.0">

    <camelContext xmlns="http://camel.apache.org/schema/blueprint">
        <route>
```

```
        <from uri="timer:first?period=1000"/>
        <setBody><constant>Hello chapter5x</constant></setBody>
        <to uri="log:main"/>
        <loop>
            <constant>3</constant>
            <to uri="direct:loop"/>
        </loop>
    </route>
    <route>
        <from uri="direct:loop"/>
        <to uri="log:loop"/>
    </route>
  </camelContext>

</blueprint>
```

This route creates a message every second and logs this message. The message is sent to a loop performing three iterations.

We start Karaf and install the `camel-blueprint` feature:

```
$ bin/karaf

karaf@root()> feature:repo-add camel 2.12.4

Adding feature url mvn:org.apache.camel.karaf/apache-
camel/2.12.4/xml/features

karaf@root()> feature:install camel-blueprint
```

We drop the `route.xml` file into the Karaf `deploy` folder. In the Karaf `log` file, we can see:

```
2014-12-16 18:19:35,000 | INFO  |  - timer://first | main | 70 -
org.apache.camel.camel-core - 2.12.4 | Exchange[ExchangePattern:
InOnly, BodyType: String, Body: Hello chapter5x]

2014-12-16 18:19:35,001 | INFO  |  - timer://first | loop | 70 -
org.apache.camel.camel-core - 2.12.4 | Exchange[ExchangePattern:
InOnly, BodyType: String, Body: Hello chapter5x]

2014-12-16 18:19:35,002 | INFO  |  - timer://first | loop | 70 -
org.apache.camel.camel-core - 2.12.4 | Exchange[ExchangePattern:
InOnly, BodyType: String, Body: Hello chapter5x]

2014-12-16 18:19:35,002 | INFO  |  - timer://first | loop | 70 -
org.apache.camel.camel-core - 2.12.4 | Exchange[ExchangePattern:
InOnly, BodyType: String, Body: Hello chapter5x]

2014-12-16 18:19:35,982 | INFO  |  - timer://first | main | 70 -
org.apache.camel.camel-core - 2.12.4 | Exchange[ExchangePattern:
InOnly, BodyType: String, Body: Hello chapter5x]
```

```
2014-12-16 18:19:35,982 | INFO  | - timer://first | loop | 70 -
org.apache.camel.camel-core - 2.12.4 | Exchange[ExchangePattern:
InOnly, BodyType: String, Body: Hello chapter5x]
2014-12-16 18:19:35,983 | INFO  | - timer://first | loop | 70 -
org.apache.camel.camel-core - 2.12.4 | Exchange[ExchangePattern:
InOnly, BodyType: String, Body: Hello chapter5x]
2014-12-16 18:19:35,983 | INFO  | - timer://first | loop | 70 -
org.apache.camel.camel-core - 2.12.4 | Exchange[ExchangePattern:
InOnly, BodyType: String, Body: Hello chapter5x]
```

We can note that the message has been processed three times by the loop route.

Message Transformation EIPs

These EIPs are extensions of the Message Translator EIP, and are dedicated to some special use cases.

The Content Enricher EIP

The Content Enricher EIP describes how to enrich the message with another system. For instance, the message contains an identifier, and you want to populate the data associated with this ID from a database.

To implement this EIP, you can use a bean or a processor as you do in the Message Translator EIP.

You can also use an endpoint that uses a transformation tool (such as `Velocity`, `Xslt`, and so on).

However, Camel provides two notations dedicated to content enrichment. They are as follows:

- `enrich` uses a producer endpoint to retrieve the data and use an aggregation strategy (like in the Aggregator EIP) to merge the data. For instance, `enrich` is used to call a webservice or another direct endpoint.

- `pollEnrich`, on the other hand, uses a consumer endpoint to poll the data and use an aggregation strategy to merge the data. For instance, `pollEnrich` is used when polling a file on the filesystem.

The Content Filter EIP

The Content Filter EIP describes how to remove part of the content of the message when the message is too large.

Camel supports this EIP by:

- Using a bean or a processor as in the Message Translator EIP
- Using the `setBody` notation containing a filter expression (such as `XPath`)

The Claim Check EIP

The Claim Check EIP describes how to replace the content of the message with a claim check (unique key), which you can use later to retrieve the message again. The message content is identified by the identifier and stored temporarily in a store such as a database or the filesystem. This pattern is really interesting to deal with very large messages that you don't want to transport to all parts of the routing.

Camel supports this EIP by combining Pipeline and a dedicated bean to store and retrieve the message using the identifier.

The Normalizer EIP

The Normalizer EIP is a combination of the Message Router EIP to deal with multiple message formats, and transform the messages into a canonical and normalized message format. One *classic* use is to transform all messages into a unique canonical format.

Camel supports this EIP by combining a content-based router and a series of beans to translate the message into the normalized format.

The Sort EIP

The Sort EIP sorts the content of the message. Basically, it applies a comparator to the message body.

Camel supports this EIP using the `sort` notation. You can provide what you want to sort (basically the body) and optionally, the comparator to use.

The Validate EIP

The Validate EIP uses an expression or a predicate to validate the content of the message. This EIP allows you to validate the payload of a message before processing it. Thanks to this, you avoid mistakes due to an invalid format.

Camel supports this EIP with the `validate` notation. The validate notation expects an expression, which is defined using any language supported by Camel.

The Messaging Endpoints EIPs

The Messaging Endpoints EIPs are related to endpoints in a Camel route. Camel supports them implicitly by using the different features provided by the endpoints.

The Messaging Mapper EIP

The Messaging Mapper EIP is actually the same thing as the Message Translator EIP, just located at the endpoint level.

In Camel, it just means that you use a bean or a processor in the same way that you do to implement the Message Translator EIP.

The Event Driven Consumer EIP

The Event Driven Consumer EIP describes an endpoint that listens for incoming messages. The endpoint reacts when it gets a message.

Camel supports this EIP by providing the components' bootstrapping endpoints that can work this way. It's the case for the CXF or JMS components, for instance.

This EIP is supported implicitly by Camel (you don't have to use any special notation).

The Polling Consumer EIP

The Polling Consumer EIP describes an endpoint that periodically polls a system (database, file system) to generate messages.

As in the Event Driven Consumer EIP, Camel supports this EIP by providing the components' bootstrapping endpoints that can work this way. This is the case for the file or FTP components, for instance.

This EIP is supported implicitly by Camel (you don't have to use any special notation).

The Competing Consumer EIP

The Competing Consumer EIP describes how to use multiple concurrent consumers on a single endpoint.

Camel supports this EIP on some components. For instance, the SEDA, VM, and JMS components support this EIP using the `concurrentConsumers` property (with a value greater than 1).

The Message Dispatcher EIP

The Message Dispatcher EIP describes how to dispatch a message to different endpoints, depending on some conditions. It's basically the same as the Message Router EIP.

Camel supports the Message Dispatcher EIP in two ways:

- Using the Content Based Router EIP (and so, the `choice` notation)
- Using the JMS component (and a message selector)

The Selective Consumer EIP

The Selective Consumer EIP describes how an endpoint can consume only some messages, based on a filter.

Camel supports this EIP in two ways:

- Using the Message Filter EIP (and the `filter` notation)
- Using a message selector on the JMS component

The Durable Subscriber EIP

The Durable Subscriber EIP describes how to use a publish-subscribe model, where the messages are stored when the subscriber is not connected, which are waiting to be delivered when they are back online.

Camel supports this EIP using the JMS component. A JMS endpoint consumer on a topic supports the `clientId` and `durableSubscriptionName` properties, allowing it to act as a durable subscriber.

The Idempotent Consumer EIP

The Idempotent Consumer EIP is used to filter duplicate messages, by identifying each message uniquely. It acts as a message filter to filter the duplicated messages. Basically, each message identifier is stored in a backend, and the EIP checks each incoming message, if it's not already present in the store.

Camel supports this EIP with the `idempotentConsumer` notation. Different message stores are available:

- `MemoryIdempotentRepository` stores the messages in a HashMap in the memory

- `FileIdempotentRepository` stores the messages on the filesystem (in a property file)
- `HazelcastIdempotentRepository` stores the messages on a Hazelcast-distributed HashMap
- `JdbcMessageIdRepository` stores the messages in a database

The Transactional Client EIP

The Transactional Client EIP describes how an endpoint can participate in a transaction. This means that it's possible that the client explicitly performs commit and rollback on a transaction. The client can be considered to be a transactional resource and can therefore manage a two-phase commit.

Camel supports this EIP by providing the components' supporting transactions. This is the case for the JMS endpoint.

The Message Gateway and Service Activator EIPs

The Message Gateway EIP describes how to wrap a message format to another message format. Basically, it wraps a Java interface as a message exchange.

Camel supports this EIP by providing components that support such wrapping, for instance, the Bean and CXF components.

Basically, the Service Activator EIP is very similar to the Message Gateway EIP.

System Management EIPs

These EIPs are not directly related to the messages. They provide a very convenient way to implement system and are useful in analyzing and managing the routing system itself.

The ControlBus EIP

The purpose of the ControlBus EIP is to be able to manage and control the routing system itself. This means being able to stop the routing system, start it again, get details about the routing activity, and so on.

Camel supports this EIP in two ways:

- Camel provides a lot of JMX MBeans, where you can find a lot of metrics and control the involved routes, processors, components, and so on.
- Camel provides a `controlbus` component that you can use to manage the Camel routes.

Using a `controlbus` endpoint, you can send a message, for instance, to stop or start a route.

The Detour EIP

The Detour EIP allows you to send messages on additional and specific steps when a control condition is met. You can use it to add extra validation, test, and debug steps when needed.

Camel supports this EIP with a message router. The condition of the message router is implemented with a bean; this bean implements the logic to define whether the detour is needed or not.

The Wire Tap EIP

The Wire Tap EIP allows you to send a copy of the message to a specific endpoint, without impacting the main route. This EIP is very useful to implement logging or auditing system.

Camel supports this EIP with the `wireTap` notation.

To illustrate the Wire Tap EIP, we create the following `route.xml` blueprint descriptor:

```xml
<?xml version="1.0" encoding="UTF-8"?>
<blueprint xmlns="http://www.osgi.org/xmlns/blueprint/v1.0.0">

    <camelContext xmlns="http://camel.apache.org/schema/blueprint">
        <route>
            <from uri="timer:fire?period=5000"/>
            <setBody><constant>Hello chapter5y</constant></setBody>
            <wireTap uri="direct:wiretap"/>
            <delay>
                <constant>3000</constant>
                <to uri="log:main"/>
            </delay>
        </route>
```

```
        <route>
            <from uri="direct:wiretap"/>
            <to uri="log:wiretap"/>
        </route>
    </camelContext>

</blueprint>
```

The first route creates a message every 5 seconds. The Wire Tap EIP sends a copy of the message to the `wiretap` route. The main route keeps on processing, using a delay of 3 seconds.

We start Karaf and install the `camel-blueprint` feature:

```
$ bin/karaf
karaf@root()> feature:repo-add camel 2.12.4
Adding feature url mvn:org.apache.camel.karaf/apache-camel/2.12.4/xml/features
karaf@root()> feature:install camel-blueprint
```

We drop our `route.xml` into the Karaf `deploy` folder. In the Karaf `log` file, we can see:

```
2014-12-16 21:41:12,553 | INFO   | ead #2 - WireTap | wiretap | 70 -
org.apache.camel.camel-core - 2.12.4 | Exchange[ExchangePattern:
InOnly, BodyType: String, Body: Hello chapter5y]
2014-12-16 21:41:15,550 | INFO   | 1 - timer://fire | main | 70 -
org.apache.camel.camel-core - 2.12.4 | Exchange[ExchangePattern:
InOnly, BodyType: String, Body: Hello chapter5y]
2014-12-16 21:41:17,540 | INFO   | ead #3 - WireTap | wiretap | 70 -
org.apache.camel.camel-core - 2.12.4 | Exchange[ExchangePattern:
InOnly, BodyType: String, Body: Hello chapter5y]
2014-12-16 21:41:20,540 | INFO   | 1 - timer://fire | main | 70 -
org.apache.camel.camel-core - 2.12.4 | Exchange[ExchangePattern:
InOnly, BodyType: String, Body: Hello chapter5y]
```

The wire tap message has been logged, whereas the main route is still on the fly. We note here that the `wire tap route` doesn't impact the main one (in terms of performances or blocking messages).

The Wire Tap EIP is especially interesting when the logging backend can take time (using a JDBC appender for instance).

The Message History EIP

The Message History EIP is used to analyze and debug the flow of messages.

Basically, it means attaching a history to a message that provides the list of all the endpoints that the message passed through.

Camel supports this EIP with the Camel Tracer feature. The Tracer is basically an interceptor on the channels; it traces all exchange details.

Due to this information, you can see where the message passed through the body of the message on each endpoint, and so on.

Every Camel route embeds the Tracer feature, but it's disabled by default. You can enable the Tracer via JMX on the route MBean.

The Log EIP

The Log EIP allows you to create a log message with all or part of the message.

Camel supports this EIP in two ways:

- Using the log component, as we did in most of the examples of this chapter
- Providing the `log` notation, allowing you to specify the log message format

To illustrate the Log EIP, we create the following `route.xml` blueprint descriptor:

```xml
<?xml version="1.0" encoding="UTF-8"?>
<blueprint xmlns="http://www.osgi.org/xmlns/blueprint/v1.0.0">

    <camelContext xmlns="http://camel.apache.org/schema/blueprint">
        <route>
            <from uri="timer:fire?period=5000"/>
            <setBody><constant>Hello chapter5z</constant></setBody>
            <to uri="log:component"/>
            <log message="Hey, you said ${body} !"
             loggingLevel="WARN" logName="EIP"/>
        </route>
    </camelContext>

</blueprint>
```

We can see here the two ways to log — using the log component or using the `log` notation.

The `log` notation (EIP) gives you complete control over what you want to log, the log level, the logger name, and possibly the log markup.

We start Karaf and install the `camel-blueprint` feature:

```
$ bin/karaf
karaf@root()> feature:repo-add camel 2.12.4
Adding feature url mvn:org.apache.camel.karaf/apache-camel/2.12.4/xml/
features
karaf@root()> feature:install camel-blueprint
```

We drop our `route.xml` file into the Karaf `deploy` folder. In the Karaf `log` file, we can see:

```
2014-12-16 21:47:34,641 | INFO  | 1 - timer://fire | component | 70 -
 org.apache.camel.camel-core - 2.12.4 | Exchange[ExchangePattern:
InOnly, BodyType: String, Body: Hello chapter5z]
2014-12-16 21:47:34,642 | WARN  | 1 - timer://fire | EIP | 70 -
org.apache.camel.camel-core - 2.12.4 | Hey, you said Hello chapter5z !
```

Here, we can see the log messages generated by the log component and the Log EIP.

Summary

We have seen that Camel supports all kinds of Enterprise Integration Patterns; from Messaging Systems EIPs to System Management EIPs, you are now ready to use the patterns that you need, and can easily implement them in your routes.

The notations are a very convenient way to describe and specify complex routing behaviors. The combination of the connectivity components and the Enterprise Integration Patterns makes Camel the most flexible and powerful routing system available.

And, if the provided components or patterns don't suit your requirements, you can always create your own specific component, as we will see in the next chapter.

6
Components and Endpoints

In the previous chapters, we have seen how to implement mediation logic and routing using processors or beans. However, both expect an incoming Exchange. It's one of the key purposes of the components and endpoints—a component creates endpoints. We have two kinds of endpoints—the producer responsible for creating Exchanges and the consumer who consumes incoming Exchanges.

The components and endpoints are responsible for:

- Interacting with the external systems and Exchanges
- Providing and handling specific data formats or transformation

To understand these concepts, we will cover the following topics:

- What are components and endpoints?
- Existing components and how to use them
- How to create our own component and endpoints

Components

The components are the main Camel extension point. Basically, a component is a factory of endpoints that you use in routes. If you take a look in the `Component` interface, you can see the following code:

```
public interface Component extends CamelContextAware {

    Endpoint createEndpoint(String uri) throws Exception;

    EndpointConfiguration createConfiguration(String uri) throws
    Exception;

    ComponentConfiguration createComponentConfiguration();

    boolean useRawUri();

}
```

You can see that a `Component` *lives* in the `CamelContext` (as it extends the `CamelContextAware` interface). This means that we instantiate a `Component` and add the instance in the `CamelContext`.

The `Component` is stored in the `CamelContext` using a unique identifier — the `scheme`. Later in the chapter, we will see that this schema is used to refer the `Component` in the route definition.

Bootstrapping a component

A component can be bootstrapped in two ways.

The first way is to explicitly instantiate the `Component`. You can do that using code.

For instance, we can explicitly instantiate the `MockComponent` and add it in the `CamelContext` using two schemes (the expected one `mock`, and a custom one `my`):

```
MockComponent mockComponent = new MockComponent();
camelContext.addComponent("mock", mockComponent);
camelContext.addComponent("my", mockComponent);
```

The second way is implicit. Camel provides a discovery mechanism that can leverage `classloader` or the IoC framework (such as Spring). Camel is searching for a file like this in `classloader`:

`/META-INF/services/org/apache/camel/component/my`

The `my` path is the component scheme name. The file contains the actual class with the component implementation. For instance:

```
class=com.packt.camel.MyComponent
```

If Camel finds the class property, it instantiates the component and adds it in the `CamelContext`. For instance, just creating the component `bean` using `blueprint` (or Spring) is enough for Camel to discover a load in the context:

```xml
<?xml version="1.0" encoding="UTF-8"?>
<blueprint xmlns="http://www.osgi.org/xmlns/blueprint/v1.0.0">

    <bean class="com.packt.camel.MyComponent">
    </bean>

    <camelContext xmlns="http://camel.apache.org/schema/blueprint">
    </camelContext>

</blueprint>
```

When used in an OSGi environment (such as in the Karaf OSGi container), Camel also looks for the components using OSGi services. This means that, in OSGi, a component exposes an OSGi service.

Currently, Camel provides more than 150 ready-to-use components:

- Some components are directly provided by `camel-core` (the low-level Camel library). For instance, `file`, `mock`, `bean`, `properties`, `direct`, `direct-vm`, `seda`, `vm`, `rest`, `ref`, `timer`, `xslt`, `controlbus`, `language`, and `log` components are directly provided (no need to install additional components).
- `camel-ahc` allows you to communicate with a HTTP service using the Async HTTP Client library from Sonatype.
- `camel-ahc-ws` allows you to communicate with a WebSocket service using the Async Http Client library from Sonatype.
- `camel-amqp` allows you to use the AMQP messaging protocol.
- `camel-apns` allows you to send notifications on Apple iOS devices.
- `camel-atmosphere-websocket` allows you to communicate with a WebSocket service using the Atmosphere library.
- `camel-atom` allows you to work with Atom feed (internally, using the Apache Abdera library).
- `camel-avro` allows you to use Apache Avro to serialize data and messages.

- `camel-aws` allows you to use the Amazon WebService service.

- `camel-beanstalk` allows you to use the Amazon Beanstalk service.

- `camel-bean-validator` allows you to validate message payload using the Java Validation API (JSR-303 or JAXP Validation and the corresponding Hibernate Validator implementation).

- `camel-box` allows you to manage files located on a `https://www.box.com/` account.

- `camel-cache` allows you to use the caching mechanism in Camel route.

- `camel-chunk` allows you to create a message using the Chunk template.

- `camel-cmis` allows you to use the Apache Chemistry Client API with CMIS.

- `camel-cometd` allows you to deliver messages using the `bayeux` protocol (using the Jetty cometd implementation).

- `camel-couchdb` allows you to interact with the Apache CouchDB database.

- `camel-crypto` allows you to sign and verify message payload using Java Cryptographic Extensions.

- `camel-cxf` allows you to use SOAP and REST web services using Apache CXF.

- `camel-dns` allows you to manipulate DNS using DNSJava.

- `camel-disruptor` allows you to use a SEDA-like component (an asynchronous queue) using the disruptor library.

- `camel-docker` allows you to deal with `docker.io`.

- `camel-dropbox` allows you to manipulate files located on a Dropbox account.

- `camel-ejb` allows you to use EJB3 as regular beans in route definition.

- `camel-elasticsearch` allows you to interact with an Elasticsearch database.

- `camel-spring` allows you to integrate a Spring application in a route.

- `camel-eventadmin` allows you to interact with the OSGi EventAdmin Layer.

- `camel-exec` allows you to execute system commands from a route.

- `camel-facebook` allows you to interface with the Facebook APIs (using the `facebook4j` library).

- `camel-flatpack` allows you to use the Flatpack library to deal with fixed width and delimited files.

- `camel-fop` allows you to render messages (in different formats such as PDF) using Apache FOP.

- `camel-freemarker` allows you to create messages using the FreeMarker template.

- `camel-ftp` allows you to consume or send files via an FTP server.
- `camel-gae` allows you to interact with the Google App Engine service.
- `camel-google-calendar` allows you to interact with Google Calendar (using the REST API).
- `camel-google-drive` allows you to retrieve or upload files on Google Drive (via the REST API).
- `camel-google-mail` allows you to retrieve or send e-mails through Gmail (using the REST API).
- `camel-gora` allows you to access the NoSQL databases using the Apache Gora library.
- `camel-geocoder` allows you to `lookup` addresses using the geolocalization.
- `camel-github` allows you to interface with GitHub.
- `camel-hazelcast` allows you to use a Hazelcast distributed queue (such as SEDA).
- `camel-hbase` allows you to interact with the Apache HBase database.
- `camel-hdfs` allows you to interact with Apache Hadoop Distributed File System (HDFS).
- `camel-hl7` allows you to deal with the HL7 MLLP protocol.
- `camel-infinispan` allows you to read and write distributed key/value pairs on Infinispan.
- `camel-http` allows you to interact with the HTTP service using the Apache HTTP Client.
- `camel-ibatis` allows you to query, insert, and update using the Apache iBatis database framework.
- `camel-mail` allows you to retrieve (using imap or pop) or send e-mails.
- `camel-irc` allows you to interact with IRC servers and channels.
- `camel-javaspace` allows you to receive or send messages using JavaSpace.
- `camel-jclouds` allows you to interact with jclouds for cloud computing and Blobstore.
- `camel-jcr` allows you to use a Content Management system such as Apache Jackrabbit.
- `camel-jdbc` allows you to perform database queries using JDBC.
- `camel-jetty` allows you to expose or use a HTTP service using the Jetty library and server.
- `camel-jgroups` allows you to interact with JGroups clusters.

- `camel-jira` allows you to interact with the JIRA bug tracker.

- `camel-jms` allows you to consume or produce messages from JMS queues or topics using a broker (such as Apache ActiveMQ or IBM MQ).

- `camel-jmx` allows you to work with JMX notifications.

- `camel-jpa` allows you to use a JPA framework (such as Hibernate or Apache OpenJPA) to interact with a database.

- `camel-jsch` allows you to use the Session Control Protocol (SCP) to download or upload files.

- `camel-jt400` allows you to use data queues from AS/400 systems (System i, IBM i, i5, and so on).

- `camel-kafka` allows you to consume or produce messages on the Apache Kafka messages broker.

- `camel-kestrel` allows you to consume or produce messages on the Kestrel queues.

- `camel-krati` allows you to interface with a Krati data store.

- `camel-ldap` allows you to query LDAP directories.

- `camel-linkedin` allows you to interact with the LinkedIn site (using the REST API).

- `camel-lucene` allows you to use the Apache Lucene search queries.

- `camel-metrics` allows you to use the Metrics library to collect activity metrics.

- `camel-mina` allows you to use the Apache MINA library to interact with different network protocols (such as Telnet and so on).

- `camel-mongodb` allows you to use MongoDB.

- `camel-mqtt` allows you to consume or produce messages through MQTT M2M brokers.

- `camel-msv` allows you to validate message payload using the MSV library.

- `camel-mustache` allows you to create or render a message using the Mustache template.

- `camel-mvel` allows you to create or render a message using the MVEL template.

- `camel-mybatis` allows you to interface with a database using the MyBatis library.

- `camel-nagios` allows you to send checks to Nagios (using the JSendNCSA library).

- `camel-netty` allows you to use TCP/UDP protocols using Java NIO (using the Netty library).

- `camel-olingo` allows you to communicate with OData 2.0 services using the Apache Olingo library.

- `camel-openshift` allows you to interact with Openshift applications.

- `camel-optaplanner` allows you to solve planning problems described in a message using the OptaPlanner library.

- `camel-paxlogging` allows you to receive log messages coming from Pax Logging (the logging framework used in Apache Karaf).

- `camel-printer` allows you to interface with printers.

- `camel-quartz` provides advanced trigger endpoints (such as the timer one) using the Quartz library.

- `camel-quickfix` allows you to receive and produce FIX messages using QuickFIX for the Java library.

- `camel-rabbitmq` allows you to consume and produce messages with the RabbitMQ broker.

- `camel-restlet` allows you to expose REST services using the RESTlet library.

- `camel-rmi` allows you to use the Java RMI service.

- `camel-jing` allows you to validate message payload using the RelaxNG compact syntax.

- `camel-rss` allows you to consume RSS feed (using the ROME library).

- `camel-salesforce` allows you to interact with Salesforce.

- `camel-sap-netweaver` allows you to interact with the SAP NetWeaver gateway.

- `camel-schematron` allows you to validate messages containing the XML document.

- `camel-sip` allows you to publish or subscribe using the Telecom SIP protocol.

- `camel-smpp` allows you to receive or send SMS messages using the JSMPP library.

- `camel-snmp` allows you to receive SNMP events using the SNMP4J library.

- `camel-solr` allows you to use an Apache Lucene Solr server via the Solrj API.

- `camel-spark-rest` allows you to easily create REST services.

- `camel-splunk` allows you to interact with applications hosted on Splunk.

- `camel-sql` allows you to perform SQL queries using JDBC.

- `camel-ssh` allows you to send commands to a SSH server.

- `camel-stax` allows you to process XML messages using SAX ContentHandler.

- `camel-stream` allows you to interact with standard input, output, and error streams.

- `camel-stomp` allows you to interact with a broker-supported STOMP protocol (such as Apache ActiveMQ).

- `camel-twitter` allows you to interact with the Twitter service.

- `camel-velocity` allows you to create/render messages using the Velocity template.

- `camel-vertx` allows you to interact with Vertx Event Bus.

- `camel-weather` allows you to retrieve weather information from Open Weather Map.

- `camel-websocket` allows you to communicate with WebSocket clients.

- `camel-xmlsecurity` allows you to sign and verify message payload using the XML signature specification.

- `camel-xmpp` allows you to work with the XMPP protocol, allowing you to work with instant messaging like Jabber.

- `camel-saxon` allows you to use XQuery on message payload (using Saxon).

- `camel-yammer` allows you to interact with the Yammer enterprise social network.

- `camel-zookeeper` allows you to interface with the Apache Zookeeper server.

The updated and complete list of Camel components is available online: `http://camel.apache.org/components.html`.

Endpoint

As we saw in the `Component` interface, the main function of a `Component` is to create an `Endpoint`. This is the purpose of the `createEndpoint()` method. This method returns an `Endpoint`. You don't explicitly call this method. The Camel routing engine calls this method for you.

When, in a route definition, you use the following syntax:

```
from("my:options")
```

During route bootstrap, the Routing Engine is looking for the my component in the `CamelContext` (loaded as explained before).

If the component is not found, we will have a no component found for scheme my message (wrapped in a `CamelRuntimeException`).

If the component is found, the routing engine instantiates the endpoint using the `createEndpoint()` method.

Let's take a look at the `Endpoint` interface:

```
public interface Endpoint extends IsSingleton, Service {

String getEndpointUri();

EndpointConfiguration getEndpointConfiguration();

Producer createProducer() throws Exception;

Consumer createConsumer(Processor processor) throws Exception;

PollingConsumer createPollingConsumer() throws Exception;

}
```

In this `Endpoint` interface snippet, we can note the following points:

- We can retrieve the endpoint URI using the `getEndpointUri()` method
- We can retrieve the endpoint configuration using the `getEndpointConfiguration()` method

The most important point is that we have different kinds of endpoints. Depending on the location of the endpoint in the route definition, Camel creates different kinds of endpoints.

If the endpoint is defined in a `to`, as follows:

```
<to uri="my:option"/>
```

The Camel routing engine calls the `createProducer()` method. The endpoint will act as a producer, meaning that the Exchange will be transformed into an external format and sent *outside* of the Camel route.

If the endpoint is defined in a `from`, as follows:

```
<from uri="my:option"/>
```

The Camel routing engine calls the `createConsumer()` or `createPollingConsumer()` method (depending on the one provided by the endpoint).

We distinguish two kinds of consumers:

- An Event-Driven Consumer (created by the `createConsumer()` method) is an Enterprise Integration Pattern. Basically, it means that the endpoint acts as a server; it waits for incoming events or messages and instantiates an Exchange for each event. For instance, CXF, Restlet, and Jetty consumer endpoints are event driven. Camel uses a thread pool—each event is processed in its own thread.

- On the other hand, a Polling Consumer (created by the `createPollingConsumer()` method) is also an Enterprise Integration Pattern. Basically, the endpoint periodically checks for a resource and instantiates an Exchange for each new resource. For instance, file, FTP, IMAP consumer endpoints are polling consumers.

We can also design a third kind of consumer, on-demand. Basically, instead of periodically polling a resource, we want to trigger the polling on demand. For instance, we want to consume a file from the filesystem when we receive an HTTP request.

To do so, we start our Karaf container:

```
$ bin/karaf
```

We install the camel-blueprint and camel-jetty features in Karaf, using the following code:

```
karaf@root()> feature:repo-add camel 2.12.4
karaf@root()> feature:install camel-blueprint
karaf@root()> feature:install camel-jetty
```

The camel-jetty feature provides the camel-jetty component that we will use in our route.

In the `Karaf deploy` folder, we create the following `route.xml` Camel Blueprint route definition file:

```xml
<?xml version="1.0" encoding="UTF-8"?>
<blueprint xmlns="http://www.osgi.org/xmlns/blueprint/v1.0.0">

  <camelContext xmlns="http://camel.apache.org/schema/blueprint">
    <route>
      <from uri="jetty:http://0.0.0.0:8181/poll"/>
      <pollEnrich uri="file:/tmp/in"/>
      <to uri="log:poller"/>
```

```
        </route>
    </camelContext>

</blueprint>
```

This route creates a Jetty event-driven consumer, waiting for incoming HTTP requests. We use the content enricher EIP through the `pollEnrich` syntax. It means that, when the Exchange is created by the Jetty endpoint, the Camel routing engine calls the file endpoint and populates the Exchange with the file consumed.

To test this route, we create the following `test.txt` file in the `/tmp/in` folder:

```
Hello chapter6a
```

Next, we just access the `http://localhost:8181/poll` URL with an Internet browser:

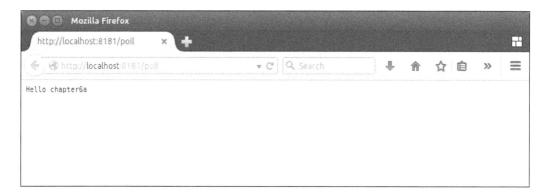

In the Karaf log, we can see the following code:

```
2015-01-06 15:00:16,291 | INFO  | qtp827039346-71  | poller | 70 -
org.apache.camel.camel-core - 2.12.4 |
Exchange[ExchangePattern: InOut, BodyType:
org.apache.camel.component.file.GenericFile, Body: [Body is file
based: GenericFile[/tmp/in/test.txt]]]
```

The file endpoint has been called *on-demand* by the `pollEnrich` syntax.

A custom component example

Even if Camel provides a lot of ready-to-use components, you might want to create your own, for instance, to support a proprietary protocol.

It's pretty easy to create our own Camel component.

In this section, we will create a component named Packt implementing a simple socket communication.

First, we create the following Maven `pom.xml` file:

```
<?xml version="1.0" encoding="UTF-8"?>
<project xmlns="http://maven.apache.org/POM/4.0.0"
xmlns:xsi="http://www.w3.org/2001/XMLSchema-instance"
xsi:schemaLocation="http://maven.apache.org/POM/4.0.0
http://maven.apache.org/xsd/maven-4.0.0.xsd">

  <modelVersion>4.0.0</modelVersion>

  <groupId>com.packt.camel.component</groupId>
  <artifactId>camel-packt</artifactId>
  <version>1.0-SNAPSHOT</version>
  <packaging>bundle</packaging>

  <properties>
      <camel.version>2.12.4</camel.version>
  </properties>

  <dependencies>
      <dependency>
          <groupId>org.apache.camel</groupId>
          <artifactId>camel-core</artifactId>
          <version>${camel.version}</version>
      </dependency>
      <dependency>
          <groupId>org.slf4j</groupId>
          <artifactId>slf4j-api</artifactId>
          <version>1.7.7</version>
      </dependency>
  </dependencies>

  <build>
      <plugins>
```

```
<plugin>
    <groupId>org.apache.felix</groupId>
    <artifactId>maven-bundle-plugin</artifactId>
    <extensions>true</extensions>
    <version>2.3.7</version>
    <configuration>
        <instructions>
            <Import-Package>
                org.slf4j;resolution:=optional,
                *
            </Import-Package>
            <Export-Package>
                com.packt.camel.component*
            </Export-Package>
            <Export-Service>
                org.apache.camel.spi.ComponentResolver;
                    component=packt
            </Export-Service>
        </instructions>
    </configuration>
</plugin>
</plugins>
</build>

</project>
```

In this `pom.xml` file, we note the following points:

- In terms of dependencies, we depend on `camel-core`, which provides the core interfaces and classes to implement components and endpoints. We also depend on `slf4j-api` just to be able to log messages.

- We use the maven-bundle-plugin to create the OSGi service for our component. This is will allow us to easily deploy the component in an OSGi container like Apache Karaf, and leverage the Camel OSGi service discovery. For that, we export the `org.apache.camel.spi.ComponentResolver` service with the `Packt` scheme.

In addition to the component discovery using the OSGi service, we also create the `META-INF/services/org/apache/camel/component/packt` file containing:

```
class=com.packt.camel.component.PacktComponent
```

The class property contains the full qualified name of the `component` class.

So, now, we have to create the `PacktComponent` class:

```
package com.packt.camel.component;

import org.apache.camel.CamelContext;
import org.apache.camel.Endpoint;
import org.apache.camel.impl.DefaultComponent;
import org.slf4j.Logger;
import org.slf4j.LoggerFactory;

import java.util.Map;

public class PacktComponent extends DefaultComponent {

  private final static Logger LOGGER = LoggerFactory
.getLogger(PacktComponent.class);

  public PacktComponent() {
      LOGGER.debug("Creating Packt Camel Component");
  }

  public PacktComponent(CamelContext camelContext) {
      super(camelContext);
      LOGGER.debug("Creating Packt Camel Component");
  }

  @Override
  protected Endpoint createEndpoint(String uri, String remaining,
    Map<String, Object> parameters) throws Exception {
      LOGGER.debug("Creating Packt Camel Endpoint");
      PacktEndpoint packtEndpoint = new PacktEndpoint(uri, this);
      setProperties(packtEndpoint, parameters);
      return packtEndpoint;
  }

}
```

Our component is pretty simple—it extends the Camel `DefaultComponent`. We just override the `createEndpoint()` method.

This method creates `PacktEndpoint`. So, we have to create this `PacktEndpoint`:

```
package com.packt.camel.component;

import org.apache.camel.Component;
```

```
import org.apache.camel.Processor;
import org.apache.camel.impl.DefaultEndpoint;

public class PacktEndpoint extends DefaultEndpoint {

  public PacktEndpoint(String uri, Component component) {
      super(uri, component);
  }

  public PacktProducer createProducer() {return new
  PacktProducer(this);
  }

  public PacktConsumer createConsumer(Processor processor) throws
  Exception {
      return new PacktConsumer(this, processor);
  }

  public boolean isSingleton() {
      return false;
  }

}
```

Our `PacktEndpoint` is the actual endpoint factory. In our component, we want to be able to create two kinds of endpoints:

- The `createProducer()` method creates a `PacktProducer` producer that we can use in a route definition with the `to` syntax.
- The `createConsumer()` method creates a `PacktConsumer` event-driven consumer, that we can use in a route definition with the `from` syntax.

Let's start with `PacktConsumer`. `PacktConsumer` extends Camel `DefaultConsumer`.

The `PacktConsumer` creates a server socket at startup. At startup, it also creates a new thread to listen for incoming client connection.

For each incoming connection (meaning a client socket connection), we create an `InOut` Exchange that we send to the next processor in the route definition. To do so, we create a Camel `DefaultExchange` using the `PacktEndpoint` and `InOut` exchange pattern.

The next processor is provided by the Camel routing engine (via `getProcessor()` method).

As we use an InOut Message Exchange Pattern, once forwarded to the next hop we are using the out message (and fallback to the in message) to reply to the client.

```
package com.packt.camel.component;

import org.apache.camel.Endpoint;
import org.apache.camel.Exchange;
import org.apache.camel.ExchangePattern;
import org.apache.camel.Processor;
import org.apache.camel.impl.DefaultConsumer;
import org.apache.camel.impl.DefaultExchange;
import org.slf4j.Logger;
import org.slf4j.LoggerFactory;

import java.io.BufferedReader;
import java.io.InputStreamReader;
import java.io.PrintWriter;
import java.net.ServerSocket;
import java.net.Socket;

public class PacktConsumer extends DefaultConsumer {

    private final static Logger LOGGER =
    LoggerFactory.getLogger(PacktConsumer.class);

    private ServerSocket serverSocket;

    public PacktConsumer(Endpoint endpoint, Processor processor)
    throws Exception {
        super(endpoint, processor);
        serverSocket = new ServerSocket(4444);
        LOGGER.debug("Creating Packt Consumer ...");
    }

    @Override
    protected void doStart() throws Exception {
        LOGGER.debug("Starting Packt Consumer ...");
        new Thread(new AcceptThread()).start();
        super.doStart();
    }

    @Override
    protected void doStop() throws Exception {
        super.doStop();
```

```
        LOGGER.debug("Stopping Packt Consumer ...");
        if (serverSocket != null) {
            serverSocket.close();
        }
    }

class AcceptThread implements Runnable {


    public void run() {
        while (true) {
            // create the exchange
            Exchange exchange = new
            DefaultExchange(getEndpoint(), ExchangePattern.InOut);
            Socket clientSocket = null;
            try {
                clientSocket = serverSocket.accept();
                PrintWriter out = new
                  PrintWriter(clientSocket.getOutputStream(),
                            true);
                BufferedReader in = new BufferedReader
                  (new InputStreamReader
                    (clientSocket.getInputStream()));
                String inputLine = in.readLine();
                if (inputLine != null) {
                    LOGGER.debug("Get input line: {}",
                                inputLine);
                    exchange.getIn().setBody(inputLine,
                                            String.class);
                    // send the exchange to the next processor
                    getProcessor().process(exchange);
                    // get out message
                    String response =
                      exchange.getOut().getBody(String.class);
                    if (response == null) {
                        response = exchange.getIn().getBody
                          (String.class);
                    }
                    if (response != null) {
                        out.println(response);
                    }
                }
            } catch (Exception e) {
                exchange.setException(e);
```

```
        } finally {
            if (clientSocket != null) {
                try {
                    clientSocket.close();
                } catch (Exception e) {
                    // nothing to do
                }
            }
        }
    }
}

}

}
```

Our event driven consumer is now ready. We now implement `PacktProducer`, which extends Camel `DefaultProducer`. A producer is pretty simple, it just overrides the `process()` method.

The `process()` method has only one argument—the Camel Exchange.

As it's a producer, the Exchange comes from a previous processor or from an endpoint. Thanks to the Exchange, we have access to the `in` message.

The following is what we do in the processor:

- We get the body of the `in` message (thanks to the Exchange).
- We create a connection to the server socket, and we send the `in` message body to this socket.
- We are waiting for the socket server response. This `in` message body is overridden by the server response.

```
package com.packt.camel.component;

import org.apache.camel.Endpoint;
import org.apache.camel.Exchange;
import org.apache.camel.impl.DefaultProducer;
import org.slf4j.Logger;
import org.slf4j.LoggerFactory;

import java.io.BufferedReader;
import java.io.InputStreamReader;
import java.io.PrintWriter;
```

```
import java.net.Socket;

public class PacktProducer extends DefaultProducer {

  private final static Logger LOGGER =
  LoggerFactory.getLogger(PacktProducer.class);

  public PacktProducer(Endpoint endpoint) {
    super(endpoint);
    LOGGER.debug("Creating Packt Producer ...");
  }

  public void process(Exchange exchange) throws Exception {
      LOGGER.debug("Processing exchange");
      String input = exchange.getIn().getBody(String.class);
      LOGGER.debug("Get input: {}", input);
      LOGGER.debug("Connecting to socket on localhost:4444");
      Socket socket = new Socket("localhost", 4444);
      PrintWriter out = new PrintWriter(socket.getOutputStream(),
                                        true);
      BufferedReader in = new BufferedReader
        (new InputStreamReader(socket.getInputStream()));
      out.println(input);
      String fromServer = in.readLine();
      LOGGER.debug("Get reply from server: {}", fromServer);
      LOGGER.debug("Populating the exchange");
      exchange.getIn().setBody(fromServer, String.class);
  }

}
```

We can now build our component using Maven:

```
$ mvn clean install
[INFO] Scanning for projects...
[INFO]
[INFO] ------------------------------------------------------------
[INFO] Building camel-packt 1.0-SNAPSHOT
[INFO] ------------------------------------------------------------
[INFO]
[INFO] --- maven-clean-plugin:2.4.1:clean (default-clean) @ camel-
packt ---
```

```
[INFO]

[INFO] --- maven-resources-plugin:2.6:resources (default-resources) @
camel-packt ---

[WARNING] Using platform encoding (UTF-8 actually) to copy filtered
resources, i.e. build is platform dependent!

[INFO] Copying 1 resource

[INFO]

[INFO] --- maven-compiler-plugin:3.2:compile (default-compile) @
camel-packt ---

[INFO] Changes detected - recompiling the module!

[WARNING] File encoding has not been set, using platform encoding
UTF-8, i.e. build is platform dependent!

[INFO] Compiling 4 source files to
/home/jbonofre/Workspace/sample/chapter6b/target/classes

[INFO]

[INFO] --- maven-resources-plugin:2.6:testResources (default-
testResources) @ camel-packt ---

[WARNING] Using platform encoding (UTF-8 actually) to copy filtered
resources, i.e. build is platform dependent!

[INFO] skip non existing resourceDirectory /home/jbonofre/Workspace/
sample/chapter6b/src/test/resources

[INFO]

[INFO] --- maven-compiler-plugin:3.2:testCompile (default-
testCompile) @ camel-packt ---

[INFO] No sources to compile

[INFO]

[INFO] --- maven-surefire-plugin:2.17:test (default-test) @ camel-
packt ---

[INFO] No tests to run.

[INFO]

[INFO] --- maven-bundle-plugin:2.3.7:bundle (default-bundle) @ camel-
packt ---

[INFO]

[INFO] --- maven-install-plugin:2.5.1:install (default-install) @
camel-packt ---

[INFO] Installing
/home/jbonofre/Workspace/sample/chapter6b/target/camel-packt-1.0-
SNAPSHOT.jar to
/home/jbonofre/.m2/repository/com/packt/camel/component/camel-
packt/1.0-SNAPSHOT/camel-packt-1.0-SNAPSHOT.jar
```

```
[INFO] Installing /home/jbonofre/Workspace/sample/chapter6b/pom.xml
to /home/jbonofre/.m2/repository/com/packt/camel/component/camel-
packt/1.0-SNAPSHOT/camel-packt-1.0-SNAPSHOT.pom

[INFO]

[INFO] --- maven-bundle-plugin:2.3.7:install (default-install) @
camel-packt ---

[INFO] Installing com/packt/camel/component/camel-packt/1.0-
SNAPSHOT/camel-packt-1.0-SNAPSHOT.jar

[INFO] Writing OBR metadata

[INFO] ------------------------------------------------------------

[INFO] BUILD SUCCESS

[INFO] ------------------------------------------------------------

[INFO] Total time: 2.105s

[INFO] Finished at: Fri Jan 09 10:59:35 CET 2015

[INFO] Final Memory: 15M/303M

[INFO] ------------------------------------------------------------
```

Our component is now ready to be deployed in Apache Karaf.

We start Karaf and install the `camel-blueprint` feature:

```
$ bin/karaf

karaf@root()> feature:repo-add camel 2.12.4

Adding feature url mvn:org.apache.camel.karaf/apache-
camel/2.12.4/xml/features

karaf@root()> feature:install camel-blueprint
```

We can now install our component:

```
karaf@root()> bundle:install mvn:com.packt.camel.component/camel-
packt/1.0-SNAPSHOT

Bundle ID: 73

karaf@root()> bundle:start 73
```

We can see that our component is now ready:

```
karaf@root()> la|grep -i packt

73 | Active    |  80 | 1.0.0.SNAPSHOT  | camel-packt
```

If we take a look at the OSGi services provided by our component, we can see the
`Component` service:

```
karaf@root()> bundle:services 73


camel-packt (73) provides:
--------------------------
[org.apache.camel.spi.ComponentResolver]
```

Camel will use this service to resolve the component associated to the Packt scheme.
To test our component, we can create the following `route.xml` Blueprint:

```
<?xml version="1.0" encoding="UTF-8"?>
<blueprint xmlns="http://www.osgi.org/xmlns/blueprint/v1.0.0">

    <camelContext xmlns=
      "http://camel.apache.org/schema/blueprint">
          <route id="server">
                <from uri="packt:server"/>
                <to uri="log:server"/>
                <setBody><simple>
                  Echo ${body}</simple></setBody>
          </route>
          <route id="client">
                <from uri="timer:fire?period=5000"/>
                <setBody><constant>chapter6b
                  </constant></setBody>
                <to uri="packt:client"/>
                <to uri="log:client"/>
          </route>
    </camelContext>

</blueprint>
```

The server route uses the Packt component to create a consumer endpoint while
waiting for an incoming connection (`from` with `packt:server`).

We can now see the Packt scheme (defined in both the OSGi service and the
META-INF service). We log the received message and return the received message
prefixed by `Echo` (using the simple Camel language).

On the other hand, the `client route` periodically creates an exchange (using timer),
and we define a `chapter6b` as the body of the `in` message (using `setBody`).

This message is sent to the server socket bound by our `server route`, using the Packt component to create a producer endpoint (`to` with `packt:client`). To deploy these routes, we just drop the `route.xml` file into the `Karaf deploy` folder. In the log, we can see the following code:

```
2015-01-09 11:58:25,758 | INFO  | Thread-16      | server | 70 -
org.apache.camel.camel-core - 2.12.4 | Exchange[ExchangePattern:
InOut, BodyType: String, Body: chapter6b]

2015-01-09 11:58:25,771 | INFO  | 1 - timer://fire | client | 70 -
org.apache.camel.camel-core - 2.12.4 | Exchange[ExchangePattern:
InOnly, BodyType: String, Body: Echo chapter6b]

2015-01-09 11:58:30,741 | INFO  | Thread-16 | server
  | 70 - org.apache.camel.camel-core - 2.12.4 |
Exchange[ExchangePattern: InOut, BodyType: String, Body: chapter6b]

2015-01-09 11:58:30,742 | INFO  | 1 - timer://fire | client | 70 -
org.apache.camel.camel-core - 2.12.4 |
Exchange[ExchangePattern: InOnly, BodyType: String, Body: Echo
chapter6b]
```

We can note that:

- The server route has been called by the client route
- The consumer prefixed the message body (with `Echo`) as defined in the simple expression

Summary

In the previous chapters, we used beans (POJO) and processors to implement mediation logic and act as a producer. However, to implement and simplify support of some protocols, systems, data transformations, and so on, Camel components are very convenient and provide easy extension points, which are ready to use in Camel route. This allows you to decouple implementation of the connectivity from the mediation logic.

Utilizing a combination of components (provided or custom), processors, beans, and route definitions provides a complete and powerful mediation framework. However, integration and mediation requires us to address a new challenge—how to handle and process errors that can happen in the mediation. This is what we will see in the next chapter.

7
Error Handling

In any integrated system, there are numerous reasons for errors to happen. Many are unforeseen, not easy to predict, and not easy to simulate. As an integrated framework, Camel provides extensive support for error handling, which is very flexible and able to deal with very different kinds of errors.

In this chapter, we will cover the following topics:

- The kind of errors that we can deal with using Camel
- The different Camel error handlers available
- The configuration of the error handlers

Types of errors

We can distinguish two main types of errors—recoverable and irrecoverable. Let's have a look at these in detail.

Recoverable errors

A recoverable error is a temporary error. It means that this error might be recovered *automatically* after a certain time.

An example would be a network connection that is temporarily down, resulting in IOException.

Basically, the exceptions are represented as recoverable errors in Camel.

In that case, Camel stores the exceptions (the recoverable errors) in the exchange using the `setException` (throwable cause) method:

```
Exchange.setException(new IOException("My exception"));
```

As we will see later, an exchange containing an exception will be caught by an error handler, which will react accordingly.

Irrecoverable errors

An irrecoverable error is an error that remains an error no matter how many times you try to perform the same action.

An example would be trying to access a nonexistent table in a database, or accessing a JMS queue that does not exist.

An irrecoverable error is represented as a message with its `setFault` flag set to `true`. The fault message is the normal message body, as follows:

```
Message msg = Exchange.getOut();
msg.setFault(true);
msg.setBody("Some Error Message");
```

Programmers can set a fault message so Camel can react accordingly and stop routing the message.

The question could be, in which case do we use an exception in the exchange and in which case do we use the fault flag on the message?

- The first reason for the presence of the fault flag is that the Camel API was designed around JBI, which includes a `Fault` message concept.

- The second reason is that we might want to handle some errors in a different way. For instance, using exceptions in an exchange will use an `ErrorHandler`, meaning that for an `InOut` exchange the next endpoint of the route won't ever get an `out` message.

Using the fault flag allows you to handle this kind of error in a specific way. For instance, with a CXF endpoint, it could make sense to create and return a SOAP fault. However, we will see that all kinds of errors can be handled by the Camel error handlers.

Camel error handlers

As we saw, Camel stores the exceptions in the exchange using the `setException(Throwable cause)` method.

Camel provides ready-to-use error handlers, depending of the mechanism that you have to implement. These error handlers will only react to the exceptions set in the exchange. By default, the error handlers won't react if an irrecoverable error has been set as the fault message. We will see, further in the chapter, that Camel provides an option to handle irrecoverable errors.

In order to react, the error handler *lives* on the route channels. Actually, an error handler is an interceptor (on the channel), that analyzes the exchange, and verifies that the exception attribute of the exchange is not null.

If the exception is not null, the error handler *reacts*. This means that the error handler will *catch* any uncaught exception thrown during the routing or processing of messages within Camel.

Camel provides different kinds of error handlers, depending on your need.

Non-transacted error handlers

The non-transacted error handlers are mentioned in this section.

DefaultErrorHandler

The `DefaultErrorHandler` is the default error handler. It doesn't support dead letter queues it propagates back to the caller. The exchange ends immediately.

It's very similar to the dead letter error handler, but the payload is lost (whereas the DLQ keeps the payload for processing).

This means that it supports redelivery policies. As we will see later, we can configure the error handler with some options.

This error handler covers most use cases. It catches exceptions in the processors and propagates them back to the previous channel, where the error handler can catch it. This gives Camel the chance to react accordingly, for instance, to reroute the message to a different route path, try a redelivery, or give up and propagate the exception back to the caller.

Even if you don't explicitly specify an error handler, Camel will implicitly create a `DefaultErrorHandler`, without redelivery, no handle (see error handlers features for details about handle), and no dead letter queue (as it's not supported by the `DefaultErrorHandler`).

To illustrate the `DefaultErrorHandler`, we create a simple Camel route that will expose a HTTP service (using Jetty).

First, we create the following Maven `pom.xml`:

```xml
<?xml version="1.0" encoding="UTF-8"?>
<project xmlns="http://maven.apache.org/POM/4.0.0"
xmlns:xsi="http://www.w3.org/2001/XMLSchema-instance"
xsi:schemaLocation="http://maven.apache.org/POM/4.0.0
http://maven.apache.org/xsd/maven-4.0.0.xsd">

    <modelVersion>4.0.0</modelVersion>

    <groupId>com.packt.camel</groupId>
    <artifactId>chapter7a</artifactId>
    <version>1.0-SNAPSHOT</version>
    <packaging>bundle</packaging>

    <dependencies>
        <dependency>
            <groupId>org.apache.camel</groupId>
            <artifactId>camel-core</artifactId>
            <version>2.12.4</version>
        </dependency>
    </dependencies>

    <build>
        <plugins>
            <plugin>
                <groupId>org.apache.felix</groupId>
                <artifactId>maven-bundle-plugin</artifactId>
                <version>2.3.7</version>
                <extensions>true</extensions>
                <configuration>
                    <instructions>
                        <Import-Package>*</Import-Package>
                    </instructions>
                </configuration>
            </plugin>
```

```
      </plugins>
   </build>

   </project>
```

The route is pretty simple. It exposes an HTTP service using the Camel Jetty component and validates the submitted message using a bean.

We write this route using the Blueprint DSL. We add the following `src/main/resources/OSGI-INF/blueprint/route.xml` file:

```xml
<?xml version="1.0" encoding="UTF-8"?>
<blueprint xmlns="http://www.osgi.org/xmlns/blueprint/v1.0.0">

  <bean id="checker" class="com.packt.camel.chapter7a.Checker"/>

  <camelContext xmlns="http://camel.apache.org/schema/blueprint">
      <route>
          <from uri="jetty:http://0.0.0.0:9999/my/route"/>
          <to uri="bean:checker"/>
      </route>
  </camelContext>

</blueprint>
```

The `checker` bean is pretty simple. It takes the message received on the Jetty endpoint and checks whether it's valid. The message is an HTTP parameter `key=value`. If the parameter has the format message=... it's valid, or else we throw an `IllegalArgumentException`.

Here's the `checker` code:

```java
package com.packt.camel.chapter7a;

public class Checker {

  public String validate(String body) throws Exception {
      String[] param = body.split("=");
      if (param.length != 2) {
          throw new IllegalArgumentException("Bad parameter");
      }
      if (!param[0].equalsIgnoreCase("message")) {
          throw new IllegalArgumentException("Message parameter
expected");
      }
```

```
        return "Hello " + param[1] + "\n";
    }


}
```

We can build our bundle using the following code:

```
$ mvn clean install

[INFO] Scanning for projects...

[INFO]

[INFO] ------------------------------------------------------------

[INFO] Building chapter7a 1.0-SNAPSHOT

[INFO] ------------------------------------------------------------

[INFO]

[INFO] --- maven-clean-plugin:2.5:clean (default-clean) @ chapter7a

[INFO]

[INFO] --- maven-resources-plugin:2.6:resources (default-resources) @
chapter7a ---

[WARNING] Using platform encoding (UTF-8 actually) to copy filtered
resources, i.e. build is platform dependent!

[INFO] Copying 1 resource

[INFO]

[INFO] --- maven-compiler-plugin:3.2:compile (default-compile) @
chapter7a ---

[INFO] Changes detected - recompiling the module!

[WARNING] File encoding has not been set, using platform encoding
UTF-8, i.e. build is platform dependent!

[INFO] Compiling 1 source file to
/home/jbonofre/Workspace/sample/chapter7a/target/classes

[INFO]

[INFO] --- maven-resources-plugin:2.6:testResources (default-
testResources) @ chapter7a ---

[WARNING] Using platform encoding (UTF-8 actually) to copy filtered
resources, i.e. build is platform dependent!

[INFO] skip non existing resourceDirectory
/home/jbonofre/Workspace/sample/chapter7a/src/test/resources

[INFO]

[INFO] --- maven-compiler-plugin:3.2:testCompile (default-
testCompile) @ chapter7a ---
```

```
[INFO] No sources to compile

[INFO]

[INFO] --- maven-surefire-plugin:2.17:test (default-test) @ chapter7a

[INFO] No tests to run.

[INFO]

[INFO] --- maven-bundle-plugin:2.3.7:bundle (default-bundle) @
chapter7a ---

[INFO]

[INFO] --- maven-install-plugin:2.5.1:install (default-install) @
chapter7a ---

[INFO] Installing /home/jbonofre/Workspace/sample/chapter7a/target/
chapter7a-1.0-
SNAPSHOT.jar to /home/jbonofre/.m2/repository/com/packt/camel/
chapter7a/1.0-
SNAPSHOT/chapter7a-1.0-SNAPSHOT.jar

[INFO] Installing /home/jbonofre/Workspace/sample/chapter7a/pom.xml
to /home/jbonofre/.m2/repository/com/packt/camel/chapter7a/1.0-
SNAPSHOT/chapter7a-1.0-SNAPSHOT.pom

[INFO]

[INFO] --- maven-bundle-plugin:2.3.7:install (default-install) @
chapter7a ---

[INFO] Installing com/packt/camel/chapter7a/1.0-SNAPSHOT/chapter7a-
1.0-SNAPSHOT.jar

[INFO] Writing OBR metadata

[INFO] ------------------------------------------------------------

[INFO] BUILD SUCCESS

[INFO] ------------------------------------------------------------

[INFO] Total time: 3.648 s

[INFO] Finished at: 2015-03-04T10:19:55+01:00

[INFO] Final Memory: 34M/1222M

[INFO] ------------------------------------------------------------
```

We now start our Apache Karaf container and install the `camel-blueprint` and
`camel-jetty` features:

```
$ bin/karaf

karaf@root()> feature:repo-add camel 2.12.4

Adding feature url mvn:org.apache.camel.karaf/apache-
camel/2.12.4/xml/features
```

```
karaf@root()> feature:install camel-blueprint
karaf@root()> feature:install camel-jetty
Refreshing bundles org.apache.camel.camel-core (60)
```

We can now install our bundle:

```
karaf@root()> bundle:install mvn:com.packt.camel/chapter7a/1.0-
SNAPSHOT
Bundle ID: 86
karaf@root()> bundle:start 86
```

We can submit a valid message using curl:

```
$ curl -d "message=chapter7a" http://localhost:9999/my/route
Hello chapter7a
```

Now, we submit an invalid message:

```
$ curl -d "foo=bar" http://localhost:9999/my/route

java.lang.IllegalArgumentException: Message parameter expected
```

In the Karaf log file (data/karaf.log), we can see:

```
2015-03-04 10:25:44,647 | ERROR | qtp766046018-75 |
DefaultErrorHandler | rg.apache.camel.util.CamelLogger
215 | 60 - org.apache.camel.camel-core - 2.12.4 | Failed delivery for
(MessageId: ID-latitude-40620-1425461026278-0-6 on ExchangeId: ID-
latitude-40620-1425461026278-0-5). Exhausted after delivery attempt:
1 caught: java.lang.IllegalArgumentException: Message parameter
expected


Message History
---------------------------------------------------------------------
----------------------------------------------------------
RouteId              ProcessorId          Processor
Elapsed (ms)
[route1]             [route1]             [http://0.0.0.0:9999/my/route]
                     [4]
[route1]             [to1]                [bean:checker]
[3]


Exchange
---------------------------------------------------------------------
----------------------------------------------------------
```

```
Exchange[
      Id                    ID-latitude-40620-1425461026278-0-5

      ExchangePattern    InOut

      Headers            {Accept=*/*, breadcrumbId=ID-latitude-40620-
1425461026278-0-6, CamelHttpMethod=POST, CamelHttpPath=,
CamelHttpQuery=null, CamelHttpServletRequest=(POST
/my/route)@132201555 org.eclipse.jetty.server.Request@7e13c53,
CamelHttpServletResponse=HTTP/1.1 200
^M
, CamelHttpUri=/my/route,
CamelHttpUrl=http://localhost:9999/my/route, CamelRedelivered=false,
CamelRedeliveryCounter=0, CamelServletContextPath=/my/route, Content-
Length=7, Content-Type=application/x-www-form-urlencoded, foo=bar,
Host=localhost:9999, User-Agent=curl/7.35.0}
      BodyType
org.apache.camel.converter.stream.InputStreamCache
      Body
[Body is instance of org.apache.camel.StreamCache]
]


Stacktrace
--------------------------------------------------------------------
------------------------------------------------------------
java.lang.IllegalArgumentException: Message parameter expected at
com.packt.camel.chapter7a.Checker.validate(Checker.java:11)[86:com.pa
ckt.camel.chapter7a:1.0.0.SNAPSHOT]
```

So we can see that the `DefaultErrorHandler` reacted for the
`IllegalArgumentException`. The delivery failed and has been logged.
By default (as handled is false), the exception is thrown back to the caller.

DeadLetterChannel

The `DeadLetterChannel` error handler implements the Dead Letter Channel EIP.
It supports the redelivery policy, and the redelivery sends the message to a dead
letter endpoint.

Even then, the dead letter endpoint, the `DeadLetterChannel` behaves like the
`DefaultErrorHandler`. To illustrate this, we update our previous example to
use a `DeadLetterChannel` that calls an error route when an exception occurs.

So the `DeadLetterChannel` error handler will catch the exception, try to redeliver,
and if it still fails the message will be sent to a dedicated route.

The `checker` bean is exactly the same as before. The route definition (using the Blueprint DSL) is different as we define the `DeadLetterChannel` error handler:

```xml
<?xml version="1.0" encoding="UTF-8"?>
<blueprint xmlns="http://www.osgi.org/xmlns/blueprint/v1.0.0">

  <bean id="checker" class="com.packt.camel.chapter7b.Checker"/>

  <camelContext xmlns="http://camel.apache.org/schema/blueprint">
      <route errorHandlerRef="myDeadLetterErrorHandler">
          <from uri="jetty:http://0.0.0.0:9999/my/route"/>
          <to uri="bean:checker"/>
      </route>
      <route>
          <from uri="direct:error"/>
          <convertBodyTo type="java.lang.String"/>
          <to uri="log:error"/>
      </route>
  </camelContext>

  <bean id="myDeadLetterErrorHandler"
    class="org.apache.camel.builder.DeadLetterChannelBuilder">
      <property name="deadLetterUri" value="direct:error"/>
      <property name="redeliveryPolicy"
  ref="myRedeliveryPolicyConfig"/>
  </bean>

  <bean id="myRedeliveryPolicyConfig"
    class="org.apache.camel.processor.RedeliveryPolicy">
      <property name="maximumRedeliveries" value="3"/>
      <property name="redeliveryDelay" value="5000"/>
  </bean>

</blueprint>
```

We can see that we use the `myDeadLetterErrorHandler` in the `main` route. The `myDeadLetterErrorHandler` is constructed using the `DeadLetterChannelBuilder` builder.

The following attributes are set:

- The `deadLetterUri` containing the endpoint is set where we send the message if the delivery fails. Here, we define the endpoint `direct:error` to call the corresponding route.

- The `redeliveryPolicy` is set to define the way we try to redeliver the message. The `myRedeliveryPolicy` defines the number of attempts (3 in the example), and the delay between each attempt (5 seconds here). It means that after 3 attempts (so, a maximum of 15 seconds), if the message still fails it will be sent to the endpoint defined in the dead letter URI (so `direct:error`, in our case).

The `error` route just logs the failed message. It means that the `main` route won't fail, it will just return the `in` message to the caller.

We build our new bundle using the following code:

```
$ mvn clean install

[INFO] ---------------------------------------------------------
[INFO] BUILD SUCCESS
[INFO] ---------------------------------------------------------
```

We start our Apache Karaf:

```
bin/karaf
```

As previously done, we install the `camel-blueprint` and `camel-jetty` features:

```
karaf@root()> feature:repo-add camel 2.12.4
Adding feature url mvn:org.apache.camel.karaf/apache-
camel/2.12.4/xml/features
karaf@root()> feature:install camel-blueprint camel-jetty
Refreshing bundles org.apache.camel.camel-core (60)
karaf@root()>
```

We can deploy our bundle:

```
karaf@root()> bundle:install mvn:com.packt.camel/chapter7b/1.0-
SNAPSHOT
Bundle ID: 86
karaf@root()> bundle:start 86
```

First, we send a valid message using curl:

```
$ curl -d "message=chapter7b" http://localhost:9999/my/route
Hello chapter7b
```

It works as before, nothing has changed.

Now, we send an invalid message:

```
$ curl -d "foo=bar" http://localhost:9999/my/route
```

We can note that curl is waiting for a response; it's normal as we defined a redelivery policy in our dead letter error handler. Finally, we receive the original in message:

```
foo=bar
```

If we take a look in the Karaf `log` file, we can see the following code corresponding to the `error` route execution:

```
2015-03-04 15:00:29,838 | INFO  | qtp1470784256-76 | error |
org.apache.camel.util.CamelLogger  176 | 60 - org.apache.camel.camel-
core - 2.12.4 | Exchange[ExchangePattern: InOnly, BodyType: String,
Body: foo=bar]
```

LoggingErrorHandler

The `LoggingErrorHandler` logs the failed message along with the exception.

Camel will, by default, log the failed message and the exception using the log name `LoggingErrorHandler` at `ERROR` level. To illustrate the behavior of the `LoggingErrorHandler`, we update the previous route `blueprint` XML like this:

```xml
<?xml version="1.0" encoding="UTF-8"?>
<blueprint xmlns="http://www.osgi.org/xmlns/blueprint/v1.0.0">
  <bean id="checker" class="com.packt.camel.chapter7c.Checker"/>
  <camelContext xmlns="http://camel.apache.org/schema/blueprint">
      <errorHandler id="myLoggingErrorHandler"
       type="LoggingErrorHandler" logName="packt" level="ERROR"/>
      <route id="main" errorHandlerRef="myLoggingErrorHandler">
          <from uri="jetty:http://0.0.0.0:9999/my/route"/>
          <to uri="bean:checker"/>
      </route>
  </camelContext>

</blueprint>
```

We define a `LoggingErrorHandler` in the `main` route. This error handler will just intercept and log the exception in the `packt` logger, with `ERROR` as the log level. The exchange ends, and the exception is sent back to the caller.

After deploying our bundle in Apache Karaf, and submitting an invalid message, we can see that the client (curl) gets the following exception:

```
$ curl -d "foo=bar" http://localhost:9999/my/route

java.lang.IllegalArgumentException: Message parameter expected at
com.packt.camel.chapter7c.Checker.validate(Checker.java:11)
```

The exception is logged in the Karaf `log` file:

```
2015-03-04 16:43:57,910 | ERROR | qtp1055249608-73 | packt |
org.apache.camel.util.CamelLogger  215 | 60 - org.apache.camel.camel-
core - 2.12.4 | Failed delivery for (MessageId: ID-latitude-41466-
1425483831913-0-2 on ExchangeId: ID-latitude-41466-1
```

```
425483831913-0-1). Exhausted after delivery attempt: 1 caught:
java.lang.IllegalArgumentException: Message parameter expected


Message History
---------------------------------------------------------------------------
-----------------------------------------------------------------
RouteId              ProcessorId        Processor
Elapsed (ms)
[route1]             [route1]           [http://0.0.0.0:9999/my/route]
[18]
[route1]             [to1]              [bean:checker]
[15]


Exchange
---------------------------------------------------------------------------
-----------------------------------------------------------------
Exchange[
     Id               ID-latitude-41466-1425483831913-0-1

     ExchangePattern  InOut

     Headers          {Accept=*/*, breadcrumbId=ID-latitude-41466-
1425483831913-0-2, CamelHttpMethod=POST, CamelHttpPath=,
CamelHttpQuery=null, CamelHttpServletRequest=(POST /my/route)@1904375366
org.eclipse.jetty.server.Request@71827646,
CamelHttpServletResponse=HTTP/1.1 200


, CamelHttpUri=/my/route, CamelHttpUrl=http://localhost:9999/my/route,
CamelRedelivered=false,
CamelRedeliveryCounter=0, CamelServletContextPath=/my/route, Content-
Length=7, Content-Type=application/x-www-form-urlencoded, foo=bar,
Host=localhost:9999, User-Agent=curl/7.35.0}
```

```
      BodyType
org.apache.camel.converter.stream.InputStreamCache
      Body
[Body is instance of org.apache.camel.StreamCache]
]


Stacktrace
---------------------------------------------------------------
---------------------------------------------------------
java.lang.IllegalArgumentException: Message parameter expected at
com.packt.camel.chapter7c.Checker.validate(Checker.java:11) [86:com.pa
ckt.camel.chapter7c:1.0.0.SNAPSHOT]
```

NoErrorHandler

The NoErrorHandler completely disables error handling; this means that any exception is not intercepted and is just returned to the caller.

For instance, if we update the Blueprint XML of our sample like this:

```xml
<?xml version="1.0" encoding="UTF-8"?>
<blueprint xmlns="http://www.osgi.org/xmlns/blueprint/v1.0.0">

  <bean id="checker" class="com.packt.camel.chapter7d.Checker"/>

  <camelContext xmlns="http://camel.apache.org/schema/blueprint">
      <errorHandler id="myNoErrorHandler" type="NoErrorHandler"/>
      <route errorHandlerRef="myNoErrorHandler">
          <from uri="jetty:http://0.0.0.0:9999/my/route"/>
          <to uri="bean:checker"/>
      </route>
  </camelContext>

</blueprint>
```

If we submit an invalid message, the exchange doesn't end, we don't have anything in the log, and the exception is just returned to the caller.

TransactedErrorHandler

The `TransactedErrorHandler` is used when a route is *flagged* with transacted.

It's basically the same as the `DefaultErrorHandler` (it's actually inherited from the `DefaultErrorHandler`). The difference is that the `TransactedErrorHandler` will look for a transaction manager.

It uses the following mechanism to find it:

- If one (and only one) bean in the registry has the `org.apache.camel.spi.TransactedPolicy` type, it uses it
- If a bean in the registry has the ID `PROPAGATION_REQUIRED` and the `org.apache.camel.spi.TransactedPolicy` type, it uses it
- If one (and only one) bean in the registry has `org.springframework.transaction.PlatformTransactionManager`, it uses it

You can also *force* the transaction manager that you want to use, as the transacted notation accepts a bean ID.

Error handlers scopes

An error handler can be defined:

- At the Camel Context level (Camel Context scope), which means that all routes in this Camel Context will use this error handler.
- At the route level (route scope), possibly overwritten the error handler defined using the Camel Context scope.

Thanks to the scope, it's possible to define a default error handler (Camel Context scope), and, possibly define an error handler specific to one particular route.

For instance, the following Blueprint XML contains two routes with two different error handlers — one with the Camel Context scope and another with `route` scope.

```xml
<?xml version="1.0" encoding="UTF-8"?>
<blueprint xmlns="http://www.osgi.org/xmlns/blueprint/v1.0.0">

  <bean id="checker" class="com.packt.camel.chapter7e.Checker"/>

  <camelContext xmlns="http://camel.apache.org/schema/blueprint"
    errorHandlerRef="deadLetterErrorHandler">
```

```
        <errorHandler id="noErrorHandler" type="NoErrorHandler"/>
        <route>
            <from uri="jetty:http://0.0.0.0:9999/my/route"/>
            <to uri="bean:checker"/>
        </route>
        <route errorHandlerRef="noErrorHandler">
            <from uri="jetty:http://0.0.0.0:8888/my/route"/>
            <to uri="bean:checker"/>
        </route>
    </camelContext>

    <bean id="deadLetterErrorHandler"
      class="org.apache.camel.builder.DeadLetterChannelBuilder">
        <property name="deadLetterUri" value="direct:error"/>
        <property name="redeliveryPolicy"
          ref="myRedeliveryPolicyConfig"/>
    </bean>

    <bean id="myRedeliveryPolicyConfig"
  class="org.apache.camel.processor.RedeliveryPolicy">
        <property name="maximumRedeliveries" value="3"/>
        <property name="redeliveryDelay" value="5000"/>
    </bean>

</blueprint>
```

Error handler features

Basically, all error handlers extend the `DefaultErrorHandler`. The `DefaultErrorHandler` provides a set of interesting features allowing you to use very fine-grained management of the exceptions.

Redelivery

The `DefaultErrorHandler` (and so the `DeadLetterErrorHandler` and `TransactedErrorHandler`) supports a redelivery mechanism that you can configure via a redelivery policy.

For instance, the following Blueprint XML creates a Camel route that systematically throws an IllegalArgumentException (with Booooommmmm message). As we don't explicitly define an error handler, the route uses the DefaultErrorHandler. We just configure the redelivery policy of the DefaultErrorHandler, trying to redeliver the message three times, waiting two seconds between each attempt. If it still fails at the fourth attempt, the exchange ends and the exception is sent to the caller.

```xml
<?xml version="1.0" encoding="UTF-8"?>
<blueprint xmlns="http://www.osgi.org/xmlns/blueprint/v1.0.0">

    <bean id="myException" class="java.lang.IllegalArgumentException">
        <argument value="Booooommmmm"/>
    </bean>

    <camelContext xmlns="http://camel.apache.org/schema/blueprint">
        <errorHandler id="defaultErrorHandler">
            <redeliveryPolicy maximumRedeliveries="3"
              redeliveryDelay="2000"/>
        </errorHandler>
        <route errorHandlerRef="defaultErrorHandler">
            <from uri="jetty:http://0.0.0.0:9999/my/route"/>
            <throwException ref="myException"/>
        </route>
    </camelContext>

</blueprint>
```

We start our Apache Karaf container and install the camel-blueprint and camel-jetty features:

```
$ bin/karaf
karaf@root> features:chooseurl camel 2.12.4
karaf@root> features:install camel-blueprint camel-jetty
```

We just drop our route.xml in the Karaf deploy folder, and we call the service using curl:

```
$ curl http://localhost:9999/my/route
```

After some time, we can see the exception (IllegalArgumentException with Booooommmmm message) returned to the client:

```
$ curl http://localhost:9999/my/route
java.lang.IllegalArgumentException: Booooommmmm
```

In the Karaf `log` file, we can see the following code:

```
2015-03-05 13:04:32,447 | ERROR | qtp307037456-75 |
DefaultErrorHandler | rg.apache.camel.util.CamelLogger
215 | 60 - org.apache.camel.camel-core - 2.12.4 | Failed delivery for
(MessageId: ID-latitude-34120-1425557044231-0-2 on ExchangeId: ID-
latitude-34120-1425557044231-0-1). Exhausted after delivery attempt:
4 caught: java.lang.IllegalArgumentException: Booooommmmm


Message History
------------------------------------------------------------------------
--------------------------------------------------------------

RouteId                 ProcessorId             Processor
Elapsed (ms)

[route1]                [route1]                [http://0.0.0.0:9999/my/route]
        [6010]

[route1]                [throwException1]       [throwException[java.lang.
IllegalArgumentException]]                                      [6007]


Exchange
------------------------------------------------------------------------
--------------------------------------------------------------

Exchange[
        Id                      ID-latitude-34120-1425557044231-0-1

        ExchangePattern         InOut

        Headers                 {Accept=*/*, breadcrumbId=ID-latitude-34120-
1425557044231-0-2, CamelHttpMethod=GET, CamelHttpPath=,
CamelHttpQuery=null, CamelHttpServletRequest=(GET
/my/route)@1911523579 org.eclipse.jetty.server.Request@71ef88fb,
CamelHttpServletResponse=HTTP/1.1 200


, CamelHttpUri=/my/route,
CamelHttpUrl=http://localhost:9999/my/route, CamelRedelivered=true,
CamelRedeliveryCounter=3, CamelRedeliveryMaxCounter=3,
CamelServletContextPath=/my/route, Content-Type=null,
Host=localhost:9999, User-Agent=curl/7.35.0}
        BodyType                null

        Body                    [Body is null]

]


Stacktrace
```


```
java.lang.IllegalArgumentException: Boooooommmmmm at
sun.reflect.NativeConstructorAccessorImpl.newInstance0(Native
Method)[:1.7.0_67]
```

We can see that the redelivery policy has been used and the exchange fails at the fourth attempt (which is exhausted after delivery attempt number four).

Exception policy

The `DefaultErrorHandler` (and so `DeadLetterChannel` and `TransactedErrorHandler`) supports the exception policy. The exception policies are used to intercept and handle specific exceptions in particular ways.

The exception policies are specified with the `onException` syntax. Camel will traverse the exception hierarchy from the bottom up to the root searching for an `onException` that matches the actual exception.

You can use `onException` with error handler defined at `CamelContext` scope or route scope. For instance, in the following `route.xml`, we have two different routes:

- The first route throws an `IllegalArgumentException` (Boooommmm)
- The second route throws an `IllegalStateException` (Kabooommmm)

We want to react differently for the two exceptions:

- For the `IllegalArgumentException`, we want to define a specific redelivery policy
- For the `IllegalStateException`, we want to redirect the message to a specific endpoint

For both exceptions, the exchange ends and the exception is sent back to the caller.

```xml
<?xml version="1.0" encoding="UTF-8"?>
<blueprint xmlns="http://www.osgi.org/xmlns/blueprint/v1.0.0">

  <bean id="illegalArgumentException"
   class="java.lang.IllegalArgumentException">
     <argument value="Boooooommmmmm"/>
  </bean>
  <bean id="illegalStateException"
 class="java.lang.IllegalStateException">
     <argument value="Kabooooommmmmm"/>
```

```
        </bean>

        <camelContext xmlns="http://camel.apache.org/schema/blueprint">
            <onException>
                <exception>java.lang.IllegalArgumentException</exception>
                <redeliveryPolicy maximumRedeliveries="2"
                 redeliveryDelay="1000"/>
            </onException>
            <onException>
                <exception>java.lang.IllegalStateException</exception>
                <to uri="direct:error"/>
            </onException>
            <route>
                <from uri="jetty:http://0.0.0.0:9999/my/route"/>
                <throwException ref="illegalArgumentException"/>
            </route>
            <route>
                <from uri="jetty:http://0.0.0.0:8888/my/route"/>
                <throwException ref="illegalStateException"/>
            </route>
            <route>
                <from uri="direct:error"/>
                <convertBodyTo type="java.lang.String"/>
                <to uri="log:error"/>
            </route>
        </camelContext>

    </blueprint>
```

We start the Apache Karaf container and install the `camel-blueprint` and `camel-jetty` features:

```
$ bin/karaf
karaf@root()> feature:repo-add camel 2.12.4
karaf@root()> feature:install camel-blueprint camel-jetty
```

We drop the `route.xml` in the Karaf `deploy` folder.

Now, if you access the HTTP endpoint corresponding to the first route, the `IllegalArgumentException` is thrown:

```
$ curl http://localhost:9999/my/route
java.lang.IllegalArgumentException: Booooommmmm
```

In the Karaf `log` file, we can see the following code:

```
2015-03-05 17:24:53,621 | ERROR | qtp486271114-76 |
DefaultErrorHandler | rg.apache.camel.util.CamelLogger
215 | 60 - org.apache.camel.camel-core - 2.12.4 | Failed delivery for
(MessageId: ID-latitude-34088-1425572554935-0-2 on ExchangeId: ID-
latitude-34088-1425572554935-0-1). Exhausted after delivery attempt:
3 caught: java.lang.IllegalArgumentException: Booooommmmm


Message History
---------------------------------------------------------------------
-------------------------------------------------------------
RouteId            ProcessorId          Processor
Elapsed (ms)
[route1]           [route1]             [http://0.0.0.0:9999/my/route]
        [2009]

[route1]           [throwException1]
        [throwException[java.lang.IllegalArgumentException]
        [2005]


Exchange
---------------------------------------------------------------------
-------------------------------------------------------------
Exchange[
    Id                 ID-latitude-34088-1425572554935-0-1

    ExchangePattern    InOut

    Headers            {Accept=*/*, breadcrumbId=ID-latitude-34088-
1425572554935-0-2, CamelHttpMethod=GET, CamelHttpPath=,
CamelHttpQuery=null, CamelHttpServletRequest=(GET
/my/route)@1882419051 org.eclipse.jetty.server.Request@70336f6b,
CamelHttpServletResponse=HTTP/1.1 200


, CamelHttpUri=/my/route, CamelHttpUrl=http://localhost:9999/my/route,
CamelRedelivered=true,
CamelRedeliveryCounter=2, CamelRedeliveryMaxCounter=2,
CamelServletContextPath=/my/route, Content-Type=null,
Host=localhost:9999, User-Agent=curl/7.35.0}
    BodyType           null

    Body               [Body is null]
]


Stacktrace
```

```
------------------------------------------------------------------
------------------------------------------------------
java.lang.IllegalArgumentException: Booooommmmm at
sun.reflect.NativeConstructorAccessorImpl.newInstance0(Native
Method) [:1.7.0_67]
```

If you access the HTTP endpoint corresponding to the second route, the
`IllegalStateException` is thrown:

```
$ curl http://localhost:8888/my/route
```

```
java.lang.IllegalStateException: Kabooooommmmm
```

In the Karaf `log` file, we can see the following code:

```
2015-03-05 17:25:02,965 | INFO | qtp1797782377-82 | error |
rg.apache.camel.util.CamelLogger   176 | 60 -
org.apache.camel.camel-core - 2.12.4 | Exchange[ExchangePattern:
InOut, BodyType: null, Body: [Body is null]]
```

```
2015-03-05 17:25:02,969 | ERROR | qtp1797782377-82 |
DefaultErrorHandler | rg.apache.camel.util.CamelLogger
215 | 60 - org.apache.camel.camel-core - 2.12.4 | Failed delivery for
(MessageId: ID-latitude-34088-1425572554935-0-4 on ExchangeId: ID-
latitude-34088-1425572554935-0-3). Exhausted after delivery attempt:
1 caught: java.lang.IllegalStateException: Kabooooommmmm. Proc
essed by failure processor:
FatalFallbackErrorHandler[Channel[sendTo(Endpoint[direct://error])]]
```

```
Message History
------------------------------------------------------------------
------------------------------------------------------
RouteId             ProcessorId        Processor
Elapsed (ms)

[route2]            [route2]           [http://0.0.0.0:8888/my/route]
                                          [7]

[route2]            [throwException2]      [throwException[java.lang.
IllegalStateException]]
            [to1]              [direct:error]
    [4]

[route3]            [convertBodyTo1]  [convertBodyTo[java.lang.String]]
                                          [0]

[route3]            [to2]              [log:error]
                                          [2]


Exchange
```

```
---------------------------------------------------------------
---------------------------------------------------------
Exchange[

    Id                 ID-latitude-34088-1425572554935-0-3

    ExchangePattern    InOut

    Headers            {Accept=*/*, breadcrumbId=ID-latitude-34088-
1425572554935-0-4, CamelHttpMethod=GET, CamelHttpPath=,
CamelHttpQuery=null, CamelHttpServletRequest=(GET /my/route)@10303

16697 org.eclipse.jetty.server.Request@3d696299,
CamelHttpServletResponse=HTTP/1.1 200


, CamelHttpUri=/my/route,
CamelHttpUrl=http://localhost:8888/my/route, CamelRedelivered=false,
CamelRedeliveryCounter=0, CamelServletContextPath=/my/route, Content-
Type=null, Host=localhost:8888, User-Agent=curl/7.35.0}

    BodyType           null

    Body               [Body is null]

]


Stacktrace
----------------------------------------------------------------
---------------------------------------------------------
java.lang.IllegalStateException: Kaboooommmmm at
sun.reflect.NativeConstructorAccessorImpl.newInstance0(Native
Method) [:1.7.0_67]
```

We can see the onException used there, redirecting the exchange to the error route.

Handling and ignoring exceptions

When handling an exception, Camel breaks out of route execution.

With a handled flag the exception is not sent back to the caller, and you can define an error message.

For instance, with the following route.xml:

```xml
<?xml version="1.0" encoding="UTF-8"?>
<blueprint xmlns="http://www.osgi.org/xmlns/blueprint/v1.0.0">

    <bean id="illegalArgumentException"
        class="java.lang.IllegalArgumentException">
```

```
        <argument value="Booooommmmm"/>
    </bean>

    <camelContext xmlns="http://camel.apache.org/schema/blueprint">
        <onException>
            <exception>java.lang.IllegalArgumentException</exception>
            <redeliveryPolicy maximumRedeliveries="2"
             redeliveryDelay="1000"/>
            <handled><constant>true</constant></handled>
            <transform><constant>Ouch we got an
             error</constant></transform>
        </onException>
        <route>
            <from uri="jetty:http://0.0.0.0:9999/my/route"/>
            <throwException ref="illegalArgumentException"/>
        </route>
    </camelContext>

</blueprint>
```

The handled flag on the `onException` prevents to send back the exception to the caller. In that case, we define an error message using a constant string.

We start Apache Karaf and install the `camel-blueprint` and `camel-jetty` features:

```
$ bin/karaf
karaf@root> features:chooseurl camel 2.12.4
karaf@root> features:install camel-blueprint camel-jetty
```

We drop the `route.xml` in the Karaf `deploy` folder. If we access the HTTP endpoint, we have:

```
$ curl http://localhost:9999/my/route
Ouch we got an error
```

On the other hand, it's possible to completely ignore an exception using the `continued` flag. For instance, with the following `route.xml`:

```
<?xml version="1.0" encoding="UTF-8"?>
<blueprint xmlns="http://www.osgi.org/xmlns/blueprint/v1.0.0">

    <bean id="illegalArgumentException"
      class="java.lang.IllegalArgumentException">
        <argument value="Booooommmmm"/>
```

```
    </bean>

    <camelContext xmlns="http://camel.apache.org/schema/blueprint">
        <onException>
            <exception>java.lang.IllegalArgumentException</exception>
            <continued><constant>true</constant></continued>
        </onException>
        <route>
            <from uri="jetty:http://0.0.0.0:9999/my/route"/>
            <throwException ref="illegalArgumentException"/>
        </route>
    </camelContext>

</blueprint>
```

We ignore the `IllegalArgumentException` thrown by the route. It means that if we access the HTTP endpoint with curl, we just have a response:

```
$ curl http://localhost:9999/my/route
$
```

This means that the `IllegalArgumentException` has been ignored, thanks to the `continued` flag.

A failover solution

The `DefaultErrorHandler` (and so the `DeadLetterChannel` and `TransactedErrorHandler`) supports routing of the failed exchange to a specific endpoint. Thanks to this mechanism we can implement a kind of failover solution, or route that could undo previous changes.

The following `route.xml` implements such a failover:

```
<?xml version="1.0" encoding="UTF-8"?>
<blueprint xmlns="http://www.osgi.org/xmlns/blueprint/v1.0.0">

  <camelContext xmlns="http://camel.apache.org/schema/blueprint">
  <onException>
  <exception>java.io.IOException</exception>
  <redeliveryPolicy maximumRedeliveries="3"/>
  <handled><constant>true</constant></handled>
  <to uri=
"ftp://fallbackftp.packt.com?user=anonymous&amp;password=foobar"/>
  </onException>
```

```
    <route>
  <from uri="file:/tmp/in"/>
  <to uri="ftp://
    ftp.packt.com?user=anonymous&amp;password=foobar"/>
    </route>
  </camelContext>

</blueprint>
```

We try to upload local files to an FTP server. If in the FTP server, an IOException is thrown, we react to the IOException (meaning that something is wrong with the FTP server), trying to redeliver three times on the same FTP server. Finally, we redirect to a fallback (another) FTP server.

onWhen

If onException allows you to filter the exceptions and react depending on the exception, it's also possible to add another condition to react to one particular exception. It's what you can do with the onWhen syntax, accepting a predicate. You have an even more fine-grained way to filter exceptions, as follows:

```
<onException>
  <exception>java.io.IOException</exception>
  <onWhen><simple>${header.foo} == bar</simple></onWhen>
  <to uri="direct:my"/>
</onException>
```

onRedeliver

The onRedeliver syntax allows you to execute some code before the message is redelivered. For instance, you can call a processor for redelivery, as follows:

```
<onException onRedeliveryRef="myRedeliveryProcessor">
  <exception>java.io.IOException</exception>
</onException>
```

retryWhile

Instead of defining a static number of redeliveries, you can use the retryWhile syntax. It allows you, at runtime, to determine whether or not to continue redelivery or to give up.

It allows you to have fine-grained redelivery control.

Try, Catch, and Finally

Until now, we have used error handlers (most of the time the `DefaultErrorHandler`), which applies to all channels in the routes. You might want to *square* the exception handling to some part of a route.

It's similar to the `try/catch/finally` Java statements.

```xml
<route>
    <from uri="direct:start"/>
    <doTry>
        <process ref="processor"/>
        <to uri="direct:result"/>
        <doCatch>
            <!-- catch multiple exceptions -->
            <exception>java.io.IOException</exception>
            <exception>java.lang.IllegalStateException</exception>
            <to uri="direct:catch"/>
        </doCatch>
        <doFinally>
            <to uri="direct:finally"/>
        </doFinally>
    </doTry>
</route>
```

Camel error handling is disabled. When using `doTry .. doCatch .. doFinally`, the regular Camel error handler does not apply. This means any `onException` or the likes does not trigger. The reason is that `doTry .. doCatch .. doFinally` is in fact its own error handler and it aims to mimic and work like `try/catch/finally` works in Java.

Summary

Generally speaking, error handling is hard. That's why Camel provides a large panel of features around error handling. Even if you can use the `doTry/doCatch/doFinally` syntax, most of the time it's better to separate the routing logic from the error handling itself.

When possible, good practice is to try to recover. It's always a good idea to use strategies for recovery. It's strongly recommended to build unit tests to simulate errors. It's what we will see in the next chapter—testing with Camel.

8
Testing

When we deal with an integration project, testing is vital to ensure that your logic works as expected. This means testing the different routing logic, and managing the errors that can happen during the routing.

Moreover, an integration project means that we use services or endpoints provided by different teams or third parties. Instead of waiting for the services and endpoints provided by the team, we can begin to implement our project by mocking the dependency services.

We can distinguish two kinds of tests:

- Unit tests are focused on testing your routing logic. Basically, it tests the behaviors of your routes.
- Integration tests are more dedicated to the installation and deployment of your routes in a container. These tests depend on the runtime container that you use to run your Camel routes.

Apache Camel provides the tool to easily implement unit tests—it's called a Camel test kit.

This chapter will introduce:

- The unit test approach and how to use the different modules provided by the test kit.
- How to bootstrap integration tests in the special case of Apache Karaf and OSGi

Unit test approach with the Camel test kit

Implementing a unit test basically means you bootstrap your routes—you load `CamelContext` and routes in the tests, and it is ready to be executed.

You now define the endpoints that you want to mock, as follows:

1. On the mocked endpoints, you define assertions.
2. Create and *inject* exchanges at some points of the routes.
3. Check whether the assertions are verified.

Camel provides different test kits, depending on the DSL that you use to write your routes:

- `camel-test` is the core and abstract test kit that you can use if you use the Java DSL.
- `camel-test-spring` extends `camel-test`, providing support for the Spring DSL.
- `camel-test-blueprint` extends `camel-test` as well, and provides support for the Blueprint DSL. Additionally, it also provides an OSGi like service support leveraging iPOJO.

All Camel test kits provide:

- JUnit extensions: JUnit is the most commonly adopted unit test framework for Java, and is freely available. Instead of reinventing the wheel, Camel directly provides JUnit extensions. This means that your unit test classes will extend the Camel JUnit extensions, and you will be able to use the JUnit annotations (like `@Test` for instance).
- Mock component: The mock component is provided directly by `camel-core`. The mock component provides a powerful declarative testing mechanism, and can be used *on top of* actual components. The declarative expectations can be created on any mock endpoint, before the test begins.
- ProducerTemplate: The `ProducerTemplate` is provided by the Camel Test base classes (or the `CamelContext`). It's a convenient feature that allows you to easily create exchanges, and set messages, which you send on the route endpoint of your choice.

ProducerTemplate

`ProducerTemplate` is a template that provides an easy way to create messages in Camel. It allows you to send message instances in an exchange to an endpoint. It supports various communication styles— `InOnly`, `InOut`, `Sync`, `Async`, and `Callback`. You can get `ProducerTemplate` from the `CamelContext`:

```
ProducerTemplate producerTemplate =
camelContext.createProducerTemplate();
```

In unit test, as soon as your test class extends to one of the Camel test base classes, you have `producerTemplate` ready to be used.

For instance, the producer template can create a message, set the body of the `in` message and send it to the `direct:input` endpoint:

```
producerTemplate.sendBody("direct:input", "Hello World", );
```

In addition to the body of the `in` message, it's also possible to set a header:

```
producerTemplate.sendBodyAndHeader("direct:input", "Hello World",
"myHeader", "headerValue");
```

The `sendBody()` method also accepts a `MessageExchangePattern` argument (if you want to simulate the `InOnly` or `InOut` exchange).

When using `InOut`, you might want to get the `out` message after the exchange execution.

In that case, you have to use the `requestBody()` method on the `producerTemplate` instead of `sendBody()` method:

```
String out =
producerTemplate.requestBody("jetty:http://0.0.0.0:8888/service",
"request", String.class);
```

JUnit extensions

Camel directly provides classes that you have to extend in your tests.

CamelTestSupport

`CamelTestSupport` is the class that you have to extend if you use the Java DSL.

You have to override the `createRouteBuilder()` method. This is where you actually bootstrap the route, by calling the `createRouteBuilder()` method defined in your route class.

You also have to override the `isMockEndpoints()` or `isMockEndpointsAndSkip()` method. This method returns a regular expression—all endpoint URIs matching this `regex` will be mocked by the mock component. The `isMockEndpoints()` and `isMockEndpointsAndSkip()` methods are the same, but the skip one doesn't send the exchange to the actual endpoint.

You are now ready to create the methods with the `@Test` annotation. These methods are the actual tests.

Here's a complete example:

```
public class MyTest extends CamelTestSupport {

    @Override
    protected RouteBuilder createRouteBuilder() throws Exception {
        MyRoute route = new MyRoute();
        return route.createRouteBuilder();
    }

    @Override
    public String isMockEndpointsAndSkip() {
        return "*";
    }

    @Test
    public void myTest() throws Exception {
        ...
    }

}
```

CamelSpringTestSupport

`CamelSpringTestSupport` is the class that your test class has to extend if you use the Spring DSL.

This is exactly the same as the `CamelTestSupport` class. The only difference is that, instead of overriding the `createRouteBuilder()` method, you have to override the `createApplicationContext()` method. The `createApplicationContext()` method actually directly loads your Spring XML file containing your route definition:

```
public class MySpringTest extends CamelSpringTestSupport {

    @Override
```

```
    protected AbstractXmlApplicationContext createApplicationContext()
throws Exception {
        return new ClassPathXmlApplicationContext("myroute.xml");
    }

    @Override
    public String isMockEndpointsAndSkip() {
      return "*";
    }

    @Test
    public void myTest() throws Exception {
        ...
    }

}
```

CamelBlueprintTestSupport

CamelBlueprintTestSupport is the class that you have to extend if you use the Blueprint DSL.

This is very similar to the CamelSpringTestSupport class, but instead of the createApplicationContext() method, you have to override the getBlueprintDescriptor() method:

```
    public class MyBlueprintTest extends CamelBlueprintTestSupport {

    @Override
    protected String getBlueprintDescriptor() throws Exception {
        return "OSGI-INF/blueprint/route.xml";
    }

    @Override
    public String isMockEndpointsAndSkip() {
      return "*";
    }

    @Test
    public void myTest() throws Exception {
        ...
    }

}
```

You can also override the `addServicesOnStartup()` method, if you want to *fake* some OSGi services used in your route blueprint XML.

The mock component

The mock component is provided by `camel-core`. It means that you can explicitly create mock endpoints with the `mock:name` URI. However, where it really makes sense to use the mock component is in unit tests—it's a cornerstone there.

Like a crash test dummy, the mock component is used to simulate real components and fake the actual endpoints.

Without the mock component, you would have to use the real components and endpoints, which is not always possible in tests. Moreover, when testing, you need to apply assertions to see if the result is as expected—we can use the mock component for that easily.

The mock component is an answer to the following situations:

- The real component or endpoint doesn't exist yet. For instance, you want to call a web service developed by another team. Unfortunately, the web service is not yet ready. In that case, you can fake the web service using the mock component.

- The real component is not easy or takes time to bootstrap.

- The real component is difficult to set up. Some components are difficult to set up, or require other applications that are difficult to set up, for instance, when you use the `camel-hbase` component in your route. This component uses an HBase instance running, meaning a running ZooKeeper and a running Hadoop HDFS cluster. It doesn't really make sense to actually use an instance HBase in unit tests (it could in integration tests). In that case, we will mock the HBase endpoint.

- The real component returns nondeterministic values. For instance, your route calls a web service that never returns the same response for the same request (for instance, containing a timestamp). It's difficult to define assertions on nondeterministic values. In that case, we will mock the web service to always return a sample response.

- You have to simulate errors. As shown in the previous chapter, it's very important to simulate errors in order to test the error handler, for instance. When we mock an endpoint, it's possible to simulate errors by throwing exceptions in mocked endpoint.

Using MockComponent

When you override the `isMockEndpoints()`, or `isMockEndpointsAndSkip()` method in your `test` class, Camel will automatically *replace* the actual endpoint with a mock endpoint, prefixing the endpoint URI with mock.

For instance, in your route, you have the file:`/tmp/in` endpoint. The `isMockEndpointsAndSkip()` method returns * meaning that all endpoints will be mocked. Camel Test creates the `mock:file:/tmp/in` mock endpoint.

You can retrieve the mock endpoint in your `test()` method using the `getMockEndpoint()` method:

```
MockEndpoint mockEndpoint = getMockEndpoint("mock:file:/tmp/in");
```

You can define the assertions on a mock endpoint:

- `expectedMessageCount(int)` defines the number of messages expected to be received by the endpoint. This count is reset and `init` at `CamelContext` creation.
- `expectedMinimumMessageCount(int)` defines the minimum number of messages expected to be received by the endpoint.
- `expectedBodiesReceived(...)` defines the expected `in` message body to be received in this order.
- `expectedHeaderRecevied(...)` defines the expected `in` message headers to be received.
- `expectsAscending(Expression)` defines the expectation of the received message order. The order is defined by the given expression.
- `expectsDescending(Expression)` is like `expectsAscending()` but in the reverse order.
- `expectsNoDuplicate(Expression)` checks that there are no duplicate messages. The duplication pattern is expressed by the expression.

Once you have defined the expectations on the mock endpoint, you call the `assertIsSatisfied()` method to validate that the expectations are satisfied:

```
MockEndpoint mockEndpoint = getMockEndpoint("mock:file:/tmp/in");
mockEndpoint.expectedMessageCount(2);
// send message with producerTemplate, see later
...
mockEndpoint.assertIsSatisfied();
```

By default, the `assertIsSatisfied()` method executes the route and waits for 10 s before shutting down the route. The timeout can be changed with the `setResultWaitTime(ms)` method. When the assertions are satisfied, Camel stops waiting and moves forward to the `assertIsSatisfied()` method call. If a message reaches the endpoint after the `assertIsSatisfied()` statement, it won't be considered. Suppose, for instance, you want to verify that no message has been received by the endpoint (with `expectedMessageCount(0)`). As, at the start, the assertion is already satisfied, Camel doesn't wait. So, you have to explicitly wait for the assertion wait time using the `setAssertPeriod()` method:

```
MockEndpoint mockEndpoint = getMockEndpoint("mock:file:/tmp/in");
mockEndpoint.setAssertPeriod(10000);
mockEndpoint.expectedMessageCount(0);
// send message with producerTemplate
...
mockEndpoint.assertIsSatisfied();
```

It's also possible to define the assertions on a specific message. The `message()` method allows you to access a specific message received by a mock endpoint:

```
MockEndpoint mockEndpoint = getMockEndpoint("mock:file:/tmp/in");
mockEndpoint.message(0).header("CamelFileName").isEqualTo("myfile");
// send message with producerTemplate
...
mockEndpoint.assertIsSatisfied();
```

The mock endpoint stores the received messages in memory. In addition to the messages themselves, it also stores the arrival time of the messages.

This means that you can define timing assertions on the messages:

```
mock.message(0).arrives().noLaterThan(2).seconds().beforeNext();
mock.message(1).arrives().noLaterThan(2).seconds().afterPrevious()
;
mock.message(2).arrives().between(1, 4).seconds().afterPrevious();
```

You can also simulate errors on a mock endpoint. It allows you to test the behavior of your route (and especially the error handler) when an error occurs.

As seen in the previous chapter, an error is actually an exception raised by an endpoint.

On a mock endpoint, you can use the `whenAnyExchangeReceived()` method to call a processor. If the processor throws an exception, we will simulate an error:

```
MockEndpoint mockEndpoint = getMockEndpoint("mock:file:/tmp/in");
mockEndpoint.whenAnyExchangeReceived(new Processor() {
  public void process(Exchange exchange) throws Exception {
    throw new IOException("Full filesystem error simulation for
                          instance");
  }
});
// send message with producerTemplate
...
mockEndpoint.assertIsSatisfied();
```

A complete example

We have a bundle with the following route using the Blueprint DSL:

```
<?xml version="1.0" encoding="UTF-8"?>
<blueprint xmlns="http://www.osgi.org/xmlns/blueprint/v1.0.0">

    <camelContext xmlns="http://camel.apache.org/schema/blueprint">
        <route id="test">
            <from uri="direct:input"/>
            <onException>
                <exception>java.lang.Exception</exception>
                <redeliveryPolicy maximumRedeliveries="2"/>
                <handled>
                    <constant>true</constant>
                </handled>
                <to uri="direct:error"/>
            </onException>
            <choice>
                <when>
                    <xpath>//country='France'</xpath>
                    <to uri="direct:france"/>
                </when>
                <when>
                    <xpath>//country='USA'</xpath>
                    <to uri="direct:usa"/>
                </when>
                <otherwise>
                    <to uri="direct:other"/>
                </otherwise>
```

```
        </choice>
      </route>
    </camelContext>

</blueprint>
```

As usual, this route Blueprint XML is located in the `src/main/resources/OSGI-INF/blueprint/route.xml` of our project.

The route logic is pretty simple:

1. We receive XML messages on the `direct:input` endpoint
2. We implement a Content-based Router EIP with the following logic:
    ○ If the message contains a country element with `France` as the value (using the `//country=France` xpath expression), we send the message to the `direct:france` endpoint.
    ○ If the message contains a country element with `USA` as the value (using the `//country=USA` xpath expression), we send the message to the `direct:usa` endpoint.
    ○ Otherwise, the message is sent to the `direct:other` endpoint.
    ○ We also configure the `DefaultErrorHandler` of the route. For all exceptions, we try:

      to redeliver the message two times

3. We set the exception handled meaning, so that we don't send back the exception *outside* of the route
4. We *forward* the *faulted* message to the `direct:error` endpoint

The `pom.xml` file of the project defines the dependencies required for the tests, especially the `camel-test-blueprint` artifact:

```
<?xml version="1.0" encoding="UTF-8"?>
<project xmlns="http://maven.apache.org/POM/4.0.0"
xmlns:xsi="http://www.w3.org/2001/XMLSchema-instance"
xsi:schemaLocation="http://maven.apache.org/POM/4.0.0
http://maven.apache.org/xsd/maven-4.0.0.xsd">

    <modelVersion>4.0.0</modelVersion>

    <groupId>com.packt.camel</groupId>
    <artifactId>chapter8a</artifactId>
    <version>1.0-SNAPSHOT</version>
```

```
        <packaging>bundle</packaging>

        <dependencies>
            <dependency>
                <groupId>org.apache.camel</groupId>
                <artifactId>camel-test-blueprint</artifactId>
                <version>2.12.4</version>
                <scope>test</scope>
            </dependency>
            <dependency>
                <groupId>org.slf4j</groupId>
                <artifactId>slf4j-simple</artifactId>
                <version>1.7.5</version>
                <scope>test</scope>
            </dependency>
        </dependencies>

        <build>
            <plugins>
                <plugin>
                    <groupId>org.apache.felix</groupId>
                    <artifactId>maven-bundle-plugin</artifactId>
                    <version>2.3.7</version>
                    <extensions>true</extensions>
                    <configuration>
                        <instructions>
                            <Import-Package>*</Import-Package>
                        </instructions>
                    </configuration>
                </plugin>
            </plugins>
        </build>

</project>
```

It's now time to implement our unit tests. We create a class at `src/test/java/com/packt/camel/test` folder, named `RouteTest.java`:

```
package com.packt.camel.test;

import org.apache.camel.Exchange;
import org.apache.camel.Processor;
import org.apache.camel.component.mock.MockEndpoint;
import org.apache.camel.test.blueprint.CamelBlueprintTestSupport;
```

```java
import org.junit.Test;

import java.io.IOException;

public class RouteTest extends CamelBlueprintTestSupport {

    @Override
    protected String getBlueprintDescriptor() {
        return "OSGI-INF/blueprint/route.xml";
    }

    @Override
    public String isMockEndpointsAndSkip() {
        return "((direct:error)|(direct:france)|(direct:usa)|(direc
t:other))";
    }

    @Test
    public void testRoutingFrance() throws Exception {
        String message =
        "<company><country>France</country></company>";

//define the expectations on the direct:france mocked endpoint
        MockEndpoint franceEndpoint =
        getMockEndpoint("mock:direct:france");
        franceEndpoint.expectedMessageCount(1);

//define the expectations on the direct:usa mocked endpoint
        MockEndpoint usaEndpoint =
        getMockEndpoint("mock:direct:usa");
        usaEndpoint.expectedMessageCount(0);

//define the expectations on the direct:error mocked endpoint
        MockEndpoint errorEndpoint =
        getMockEndpoint("mock:direct:error");
        errorEndpoint.expectedMessageCount(0);

//define the expectations on the direct:other mocked endpoint
        MockEndpoint otherEndpoint =
        getMockEndpoint("mock:direct:other");
        otherEndpoint.expectedMessageCount(0);

//sending the message in the direct:input mocked endpoint
        template.sendBody("direct:input", message);
```

```
//validate the expectations
      assertMockEndpointsSatisfied();
  }
  @Test
  public void testRoutingUsa() throws Exception {
      String message =
      "<company><country>USA</country></company>";

//define the expectations on the direct:france mocked endpoint
      MockEndpoint franceEndpoint =
      getMockEndpoint("mock:direct:france");
      franceEndpoint.expectedMessageCount(0);

//define the expectations on the direct:usa mocked endpoint
      MockEndpoint usaEndpoint =
      getMockEndpoint("mock:direct:usa");
      usaEndpoint.expectedMessageCount(1);

//define the expectations on the direct:error mocked endpoint
      MockEndpoint errorEndpoint =
      getMockEndpoint("mock:direct:error");
      errorEndpoint.expectedMessageCount(0);

//define the expectations on the direct:other mocked endpoint
      MockEndpoint otherEndpoint =
      getMockEndpoint("mock:direct:other");
      otherEndpoint.expectedMessageCount(0);

//sending the message in the direct:input mocked endpoint
      template.sendBody("direct:input", message);

//validate the expectations
      assertMockEndpointsSatisfied();
  }

  @Test
  public void testRoutingOther() throws Exception {
      String message =
      "<company><country>Spain</country></company>";

//define the expectations on the direct:france mocked endpoint
      MockEndpoint franceEndpoint =
      getMockEndpoint("mock:direct:france");
      franceEndpoint.expectedMessageCount(0);
```

```
//define the expectations on the direct:usa mocked endpoint
    MockEndpoint usaEndpoint =
    getMockEndpoint("mock:direct:usa");
    usaEndpoint.expectedMessageCount(0);

//define the expectations on the direct:error mocked endpoint
    MockEndpoint errorEndpoint =
    getMockEndpoint("mock:direct:error");
    errorEndpoint.expectedMessageCount(0);

//define the expectations on the direct:other mocked endpoint
    MockEndpoint otherEndpoint =
    getMockEndpoint("mock:direct:other");
    otherEndpoint.expectedMessageCount(1);

//sending the message in the direct:input mocked endpoint
    template.sendBody("direct:input", message);

//validate the expectations
    assertMockEndpointsSatisfied();
  }

  @Test
  public void testError() throws Exception {
      String message =
      "<company><country>France</country></company>";

// fake an error on the direct:france mocked endpoint
    MockEndpoint franceEndpoint =
    getMockEndpoint("mock:direct:france");
    franceEndpoint.whenAnyExchangeReceived(new Processor() {
        public void process(Exchange exchange) throws
        Exception {
            throw new IOException("Simulated error");
        }
    });

  //define the expectations on the direct:usa mocked endpoint
    MockEndpoint usaEndpoint =
    getMockEndpoint("mock:direct:usa");
    usaEndpoint.expectedMessageCount(0);

//define the expectations on the direct:error mocked endpoint
    MockEndpoint errorEndpoint =
    getMockEndpoint("mock:direct:error");
```

```
        errorEndpoint.expectedMessageCount(1);

    //define the expectations on the direct:other mocked endpoint
        MockEndpoint otherEndpoint =
        getMockEndpoint("mock:direct:other");
        otherEndpoint.expectedMessageCount(0);

    //sending the message in the direct:input mocked endpoint
        template.sendBody("direct:input", message);

        // validate the expectations
        assertMockEndpointsSatisfied();
    }


}
```

This class extends the `CamelBlueprintTestSupport` class, as our route is written using the Blueprint DSL. Before actually implementing the tests, we have to *bootstrap* the test.

The first step is to load the Blueprint XML. For that, we override the `getBlueprintDescriptor()` method. This method just returns the location of the Blueprint XML file.

The second step is to define the endpoints that we want to mock. So we override the `isMockEndpointsAndSkip()` method. This method returns a regular expression for the endpoints URI to match. Camel will mock the corresponding endpoints and won't send the message to the actual endpoints. Here, we want to mock all *outbound* endpoints of the routes—`direct:error`, `direct:france`, `direct:usa`, and `direct:other`. We don't want to mock the `direct:input` *inbound* endpoint, as we will use the producer template to send an exchange there.

We are now ready to implement the unit tests.

The tests are implemented by method annotation with `@Test`.

The first test method is `testRoutingFrance()`. This test:

- Creates an XML message containing an element country with `France` as the value
- On the mocked `direct:france` endpoint, we expect to receive one message, according to the ContentBasedRouter EIP
- On the mocked `direct:usa` endpoint, we expect to receive no message
- On the mocked `direct:error` endpoint, we expect to receive no message

- On the mocked `direct:other` endpoint, we expect to receive no message
- We use the producer template to send the XML message to the `direct:input` endpoint
- Once the message has been sent, we check if the expectations are satisfied

The second test method is `testRoutingUsa()`. This test is basically the same as the `testRoutingFrance()` method. However, we want to test the `ContentBasedRouter` with an XML message containing the `<country/>` element with the USA value. We update the expectations on the different mocked endpoints.

The third test method is `testRoutingOther()`. This test is basically the same as the two previous methods. However, we want to test the `ContentBasedRouter` with an XML message containing the `<country/>` element with the `Spain` value. We update the expectations accordingly.

We also want to test our `DefaultErrorHandling`. So, we want to simulate an error to see if the error handler reacts as expected.

To fake an error, we add a processor on the mocked `direct:france` endpoint. This processor throws an `IOException`. This exception will be caught by the error handler.

As the error handler *forwards* the message to the `direct:error` endpoint, we can define the expectations on the mocked `direct:error` to be sure that the endpoint received the *failed* message (forwarded by the error handler).

To execute our tests, we just run:

```
$ mvn clean test
```

```
[main] INFO org.apache.camel.blueprint.BlueprintCamelContext - Apache
Camel 2.12.4 (CamelContext: 22-camel-12) is starting

[main] INFO org.apache.camel.management.DefaultManagementStrategy -
JMX is disabled

[main] INFO org.apache.camel.impl.InterceptSendToMockEndpointStrategy
- Adviced endpoint [direct://error] with mock endpoint
[mock:direct:error]

[main] INFO org.apache.camel.impl.InterceptSendToMockEndpointStrategy
- Adviced endpoint [direct://france] with mock endpoint
[mock:direct:france]

[main] INFO org.apache.camel.impl.InterceptSendToMockEndpointStrategy
- Adviced endpoint [direct://usa] with mock endpoint
[mock:direct:usa]

[main] INFO org.apache.camel.impl.InterceptSendToMockEndpointStrategy
```

- Adviced endpoint [direct://other] with mock endpoint
[mock:direct:other]

[main] INFO org.apache.camel.blueprint.BlueprintCamelContext -
AllowUseOriginalMessage is enabled. If access to the original message
is not needed, then its recommended to turn this option off as it may
improve performance.

[main] INFO org.apache.camel.blueprint.BlueprintCamelContext -
StreamCaching is not in use. If using streams then its recommended to
enable stream caching. See more details at
http://camel.apache.org/stream-caching.html

[main] INFO org.apache.camel.blueprint.BlueprintCamelContext - Route:
test started and consuming from: Endpoint[direct://input]

[main] INFO org.apache.camel.blueprint.BlueprintCamelContext - Total
1 routes, of which 1 is started.

[main] INFO org.apache.camel.blueprint.BlueprintCamelContext - Apache
Camel 2.12.4 (CamelContext: 22-camel-12) started in 0.015 seconds

[main] INFO org.apache.camel.component.mock.MockEndpoint - Asserting:
Endpoint[mock://direct:france] is satisfied

[main] INFO org.apache.camel.component.mock.MockEndpoint - Asserting:
Endpoint[mock://direct:usa] is satisfied

[main] INFO org.apache.camel.component.mock.MockEndpoint - Asserting:
Endpoint[mock://direct:error] is satisfied

[main] INFO org.apache.camel.component.mock.MockEndpoint - Asserting:
Endpoint[mock://direct:other] is satisfied

[main] INFO com.packt.camel.test.RouteTest -
****
****

[main] INFO com.packt.camel.test.RouteTest - Testing done:
testRoutingOther(com.packt.camel.test.RouteTest)

[main] INFO com.packt.camel.test.RouteTest - Took: 0.021 seconds (21
millis)

[main] INFO com.packt.camel.test.RouteTest -
****
****

[main] INFO org.apache.camel.blueprint.BlueprintCamelContext - Apache
Camel 2.12.4 (CamelContext: 22-camel-12) is shutting down

[main] INFO org.apache.camel.impl.DefaultShutdownStrategy - Starting
to graceful shutdown 1 routes (timeout 10 seconds)

[Camel (22-camel-12) thread #3 - ShutdownTask] INFO
org.apache.camel.impl.DefaultShutdownStrategy - Route: test shutdown
complete, was consuming from: Endpoint[direct://input]

```
[main] INFO org.apache.camel.impl.DefaultShutdownStrategy - Graceful
shutdown of 1 routes completed in 0 seconds

[main] INFO org.apache.camel.blueprint.BlueprintCamelContext - Apache
Camel 2.12.4 (CamelContext: 22-camel-12) uptime 0.024 seconds

[main] INFO org.apache.camel.blueprint.BlueprintCamelContext - Apache
Camel 2.12.4 (CamelContext: 22-camel-12) is shutdown in 0.002 seconds

[main] INFO org.apache.aries.blueprint.container.BlueprintExtender -
Destroying BlueprintContainer for bundle RouteTest

[main] INFO org.apache.aries.blueprint.container.BlueprintExtender -
Destroying BlueprintContainer for bundle org.apache.aries.blueprint

[main] INFO org.apache.aries.blueprint.container.BlueprintExtender -
Destroying BlueprintContainer for bundle org.apache.camel.camel-
blueprint

[main] INFO org.apache.camel.impl.osgi.Activator - Camel activator
stopping

[main] INFO org.apache.camel.impl.osgi.Activator - Camel activator
stopped

[main] INFO org.apache.camel.test.blueprint.CamelBlueprintHelper -
Deleting work directory target/bundles/1427661985280

Tests run: 4, Failures: 0, Errors: 0, Skipped: 0, Time elapsed: 3.025
sec - in com.packt.camel.test.RouteTest


Results :


Tests run: 4, Failures: 0, Errors: 0, Skipped: 0


[INFO] -------------------------------------------------------------
[INFO] BUILD SUCCESS
[INFO] -------------------------------------------------------------
[INFO] Total time: 4.842 s
[INFO] Finished at: 2015-03-29T22:46:25+02:00
[INFO] Final Memory: 18M/303M
```

We can see the different mock endpoints created by Camel in the output messages, (for instance `[main] INFO org.apache.camel.component.mock.MockEndpoint - Asserting: Endpoint[mock://direct:other]` is satisfied).

Additional annotations

The Camel test kit also provides additional annotations, in order to simplify the code of your tests.

Instead of using the `getMockEndpoint()` method to get the mocked endpoints, you can use the `@EndpointInject` annotation:

```
@EndpointInject(uri = "mock:direct:france")
protected MockEndpoint franceEndpoint;
```

Now, we can directly use the `franceEndpoint` mock endpoint in the test methods:

```
@Test
public void aTest() throws Exception {
  ...
  franceEndpoint.expectedBodiesReceived("<foo/>");
  ...
  franceEndpoint.assertIsSatisfied();
}
```

Similarly, instead of defining the endpoint URI on the producer template, you can use the `@Producer` annotation to define where the producer template sends the message:

```
@Produce(uri = "direct:input");
protected ProducerTemplate template;
```

We can now directly use the producer template without specifying the endpoint:

```
@Test
public void aTest() throws Exception {
  ...
  template.sendBodyAndHeader("<message/>", "foo", "bar");

}
```

Mocking OSGi services

The Camel Blueprint test kit allows you to mock and prototype OSGi services.

For that, the kit uses the `PojoSR` library.

For instance, we want to test the following route:

```xml
<?xml version="1.0" encoding="UTF-8"?>
<blueprint xmlns="http://www.osgi.org/xmlns/blueprint/v1.0.0">

    <reference id="service" interface="org.apache.camel.Processor"/>

    <camelContext xmlns="http://camel.apache.org/schema/blueprint">
        <route id="test">
            <from uri="direct:input"/>
            <process ref="service"/>
            <to uri="direct:output"/>
        </route>
    </camelContext>

</blueprint>
```

If this route is very simple, it uses an OSGi service via the `<reference/>` element. In the OSGi container, the reference element is looking for the actual service in the OSGi Service Registry.

Instead of using a real blueprint container, the Camel Blueprint test kit allows you to register services. For that, we just override the `addServicesOnStartup()` method where we add the bean providing the services used in the route.

The test class is as follows:

```java
package com.packt.camel.test;

import org.apache.camel.Exchange; import org.apache.camel.Processor;
import org.apache.camel.component.mock.MockEndpoint;
import org.apache.camel.test.blueprint.CamelBlueprintTestSupport;
import org.apache.camel.util.KeyValueHolder;
import org.junit.Test;

import java.util.Dictionary;
import java.util.Map;

public class RouteTest extends CamelBlueprintTestSupport {

    @Override
    protected String getBlueprintDescriptor() {
        return "OSGI-INF/blueprint/route.xml";
    }
```

```
    @Override
    public String isMockEndpointsAndSkip() {
        return "direct:output";
    }

    @Override
    public void addServicesOnStartup(Map<String,
    KeyValueHolder<Object, Dictionary>> services) {
        KeyValueHolder serviceHolder = new KeyValueHolder(new
                                         Processor() {
            public void process(Exchange exchange) throws
            Exception {
                exchange.getIn().setBody("DONE", String.class);
            }
        }, null);
        services.put(Processor.class.getName(), serviceHolder);
    }

    @Test
    public void testRoute() throws Exception {
        String message = "BEGIN";

        MockEndpoint franceEndpoint =
        getMockEndpoint("mock:direct:output");
        franceEndpoint.expectedMessageCount(1);
        franceEndpoint.expectedBodiesReceived("DONE");

        template.sendBody("direct:input", message);

        assertMockEndpointsSatisfied();
    }
}
```

We can see that we define the mocked service directly in the test. As for the previous test, we execute the test with:

```
$ mvn clean test
```

```
[main] INFO org.apache.aries.blueprint.container.BlueprintExtender -
No quiesce support is available, so blueprint components will not
participate in quiesce operations
```

```
[main] INFO com.packt.camel.test.RouteTest -
**********************************************************************

[main] INFO com.packt.camel.test.RouteTest - Testing:
testService(com.packt.camel.test.RouteTest)

[main] INFO com.packt.camel.test.RouteTest -
**********************************************************************

[Blueprint Extender: 3] INFO
org.apache.aries.blueprint.container.BlueprintContainerImpl - Bundle
RouteTest is waiting for namespace handlers
[http://camel.apache.org/schema/blueprint]

[main] INFO com.packt.camel.test.RouteTest - Skipping starting
CamelContext as system property skipStartingCamelContext is set to be
true.

[main] INFO org.apache.camel.blueprint.BlueprintCamelContext - Apache
Camel 2.12.4 (CamelContext: 22-camel-3) is starting

[main] INFO org.apache.camel.management.DefaultManagementStrategy -
JMX is disabled

[main] INFO org.apache.camel.impl.InterceptSendToMockEndpointStrategy
- Adviced endpoint [direct://output] with mock endpoint
[mock:direct:output]

[main] INFO org.apache.camel.blueprint.BlueprintCamelContext -
AllowUseOriginalMessage is enabled. If access to the original message
is not needed, then its recommended to turn this option off as it may
improve performance.

[main] INFO org.apache.camel.blueprint.BlueprintCamelContext -
StreamCaching is not in use. If using streams then its recommended to
enable stream caching. See more details at
http://camel.apache.org/stream-caching.html

[main] INFO org.apache.camel.blueprint.BlueprintCamelContext - Route:
test started and consuming from: Endpoint[direct://input]

[main] INFO org.apache.camel.blueprint.BlueprintCamelContext - Total
1 routes, of which 1 is started.

[main] INFO org.apache.camel.blueprint.BlueprintCamelContext - Apache
Camel 2.12.4 (CamelContext: 22-camel-3) started in 0.050 seconds

[main] INFO org.apache.camel.component.mock.MockEndpoint - Asserting:
Endpoint[mock://direct:output] is satisfied

[main] INFO com.packt.camel.test.RouteTest -
**********************************************************************

[main] INFO com.packt.camel.test.RouteTest - Testing done:
testService(com.packt.camel.test.RouteTest)

[main] INFO com.packt.camel.test.RouteTest - Took: 0.062 seconds (62
millis)
```

```
[main] INFO com.packt.camel.test.RouteTest -
**********************************************************************

[main] INFO org.apache.camel.blueprint.BlueprintCamelContext - Apache
Camel 2.12.4 (CamelContext: 22-camel-3) is shutting down

[main] INFO org.apache.camel.impl.DefaultShutdownStrategy - Starting
to graceful shutdown 1 routes (timeout 10 seconds)

[Camel (22-camel-3) thread #0 - ShutdownTask] INFO
org.apache.camel.impl.DefaultShutdownStrategy - Route: test shutdown
complete, was consuming from: Endpoint[direct://input]

[main] INFO org.apache.camel.impl.DefaultShutdownStrategy - Graceful
shutdown of 1 routes completed in 0 seconds

[main] INFO org.apache.camel.blueprint.BlueprintCamelContext - Apache
Camel 2.12.4 (CamelContext: 22-camel-3) uptime 0.070 seconds

[main] INFO org.apache.camel.blueprint.BlueprintCamelContext - Apache
Camel 2.12.4 (CamelContext: 22-camel-3) is shutdown in 0.007 seconds

[main] INFO org.apache.aries.blueprint.container.BlueprintExtender -
Destroying BlueprintContainer for bundle RouteTest

[main] INFO org.apache.aries.blueprint.container.BlueprintExtender -
Destroying BlueprintContainer for bundle org.apache.aries.blueprint

[main] INFO org.apache.aries.blueprint.container.BlueprintExtender -
Destroying BlueprintContainer for bundle org.apache.camel.camel-
blueprint

[main] INFO org.apache.camel.impl.osgi.Activator - Camel activator
stopping

[main] INFO org.apache.camel.impl.osgi.Activator - Camel activator
stopped

[main] INFO org.apache.camel.test.blueprint.CamelBlueprintHelper -
Deleting work directory target/bundles/1427662210482

Tests run: 1, Failures: 0, Errors: 0, Skipped: 0, Time elapsed: 1.744
sec - in com.packt.camel.test.RouteTest


Results :


Tests run: 1, Failures: 0, Errors: 0, Skipped: 0


[INFO] ------------------------------------------------------------
[INFO] BUILD SUCCESS
[INFO] ------------------------------------------------------------
[INFO] Total time: 3.573 s
[INFO] Finished at: 2015-03-29T22:50:12+02:00
```

```
[INFO] Final Memory: 18M/303M
[INFO] ----------------------------------------------------------------
```

As we saw in this chapter, the Camel test kits allow you to easily prototype services and endpoints, and test your routes.

Tests are really important to guarantee the integration logic implemented, and also to be sure that the error handler and routing react as you expect.

Summary

As we see in this chapter, Camel provides rich features allowing you to easily implement unit tests and integration tests.

Thanks to that, you can test the integration logic that you want to implement in your routes, and you can also move forward in your implementation, by mocking parts of your integration logic.

With such tests, you can use test driven implementation, where you start by implementing the test with your expectation, and implement your routes based on these expectations.

Index

Symbols

@Bean annotation 53
@BeanShell annotation 54
@Constant annotation 54
@EL annotation 54
@Groovy annotation 54
@JavaScript annotation 54
@MVEL annotation 54
@OGNL annotation 54
@PHP annotation 55
@Python annotation 55
@Ruby annotation 55
@Simple annotation 55
@XPath annotation 55
@XQuery annotation 55

A

annotations, expression languages
  about 52, 53
  @Bean 53
  @Constant 54
  @EL 54
  @Groovy 54
  @JavaScript 54
  @MVEL 54
  @OGNL 54
  @PHP 55
  @Python 55
  @Simple 55
  @XPath 55
  @XQuery 55
Apache Camel, features
  active community 6
  component, and bean support 3

  deployment topologies 5
  easy configuration 4
  expressions 4
  Java Management Extension (JMX), using 6
  lightweight 5
  predicates 3
  quick prototyping 5, 6
  testing support 5, 6
  type conversion 4
  URI 4
Apache ServiceMix 3 1
ApplicationContextRegistry 46

B

bean
  method bindings 50, 51
  MyBean class, creating 57, 58
  route definition, writing with Camel
      Blueprint DSL 58, 59
  used, for creating OSGi bundle 56, 57

C

Camel
  components 138
  endpoint 144
  error handlers 163
  routes, containing processors 22, 23
Camel Blueprint DSL
  used, for creating routes 27-35
  used, for writing route definition 58
Camel context
  about 11
  contents 12, 13

method bindings
  bean 50, 51
mock component
  about 194-196
  assertions, defining 195
MyBean class
  creating 57
  doMyLogic() method 57
  setMyHeader() method 57

N

non-transacted error handlers
  about 163
  DeadLetterChannel 169-172
  DefaultErrorHandler 163-169
  LoggingErrorHandler 172
  NoErrorHandler 174
Normalized Messages Router (NMR) 2

O

OSGi bundle
  about 22
  building 59-64
  creating, with bean 56, 57
  deploying 59-64
OsgiServiceRegistry 46
OSGi services
  mocking 207-212

P

Pipeline EIP
  about 67
  explicit pipeline 71-73
  implicit pipeline 68-70
  Message Router EIP 73, 74
Polling Consumers 17
processor 13, 14, 22
producer 17

R

registry
  about 39, 40
  ApplicationContextRegistry 46
  CompositeRegistry 46
  JndiRegistry 43-46
  OsgiServiceRegistry 46
  SimpleRegistry 40-43
requestBody() method 191
routes 14

S

service activator 50
setMyHeader() method 59
shutdown strategy
  phases 13
SimpleRegistry 40-43
System Management EIPs
  ControlBus EIP 132
  Detour EIP 133
  Log EIP 135, 136
  Message History EIP 135
  Wire Tap EIP 133, 134

T

tests
  integration tests 189
  unit tests 189
TransactedErrorHandler 175
type converter
  about 19
  destination type 19
  source type 19

U

unit test
  Camel test kit, using 190

W

WebService Description Language
    (WSDL) 1

Thank you for buying
Mastering Apache Camel

About Packt Publishing

Packt, pronounced 'packed', published its first book, *Mastering phpMyAdmin for Effective MySQL Management*, in April 2004, and subsequently continued to specialize in publishing highly focused books on specific technologies and solutions.

Our books and publications share the experiences of your fellow IT professionals in adapting and customizing today's systems, applications, and frameworks. Our solution-based books give you the knowledge and power to customize the software and technologies you're using to get the job done. Packt books are more specific and less general than the IT books you have seen in the past. Our unique business model allows us to bring you more focused information, giving you more of what you need to know, and less of what you don't.

Packt is a modern yet unique publishing company that focuses on producing quality, cutting-edge books for communities of developers, administrators, and newbies alike. For more information, please visit our website at www.packtpub.com.

About Packt Enterprise

In 2010, Packt launched two new brands, Packt Enterprise and Packt Open Source, in order to continue its focus on specialization. This book is part of the Packt Enterprise brand, home to books published on enterprise software – software created by major vendors, including (but not limited to) IBM, Microsoft, and Oracle, often for use in other corporations. Its titles will offer information relevant to a range of users of this software, including administrators, developers, architects, and end users.

Writing for Packt

We welcome all inquiries from people who are interested in authoring. Book proposals should be sent to author@packtpub.com. If your book idea is still at an early stage and you would like to discuss it first before writing a formal book proposal, then please contact us; one of our commissioning editors will get in touch with you.

We're not just looking for published authors; if you have strong technical skills but no writing experience, our experienced editors can help you develop a writing career, or simply get some additional reward for your expertise.

Quick answers to common problems

Apache Camel Developer's Cookbook

Solve common integration tasks with over 100 easily accessible Apache Camel recipes

Scott Cranton   Jakub Korab   [PACKT] enterprise ⊠

Apache Camel Developer's Cookbook

ISBN: 978-1-78217-030-3   Paperback: 424 pages

Solve common integration tasks with over 100 easily accessible Apache Camel recipes

1. A practical guide to using Apache Camel delivered in dozens of small, useful recipes.

2. Written in a Cookbook format that allows you to quickly look up the features you need, delivering the most important steps to perform with a brief follow-on explanation of what's happening under the covers.

3. The recipes cover the full range of Apache Camel usage from creating initial integrations, transformations and routing, debugging, monitoring, security, and more.

INSTANT
Short | Fast | Focused

Apache Camel Messaging System

Tackle integration problems and learn practical ways to make data flow between your application and other systems using Apache Camel

Evgeniy Sharapov   [PACKT]

Instant Apache Camel Messaging System

ISBN: 978-1-78216-534-7   Paperback: 78 pages

Tackle integration problems and learn practical ways to make data flow between your application and other systems using Apache Camel

1. Learn something new in an Instant! A short, fast, focused guide delivering immediate results.

2. Use Apache Camel to connect your application to different systems.

3. Test your Camel application using unit tests, mocking, and component substitution.

4. Configure your Apache Camel application using the Spring Framework.

Please check **www.PacktPub.com** for information on our titles

Instant Apache Camel Message Routing

ISBN: 978-1-78328-347-7   Paperback: 62 pages

Route, transform, split, multicast messages, and do much more with Camel

1. Learn something new in an Instant! A short, fast, focused guide delivering immediate results.

2. Learn how to use Enterprise Integration Patterns for message routing.

3. Learn how Camel works and how it integrates disparate systems.

4. Learn how to test and monitor Camel applications.

Apache Karaf Cookbook

ISBN: 978-1-78398-508-1   Paperback: 260 pages

Over 60 recipes to help you get the most out of your Apache Karaf deployments

1. Leverage Apache Karaf to apply OSGi's powerful features to frameworks such as Apache ActiveMQ, Camel, Cassandra, CXF, and Hadoop.

2. Set up Apache Karaf for high availability.

3. A thorough guide with example-based recipes to help you get a deeper understanding of Apache Karaf's capabilities.

Please check **www.PacktPub.com** for information on our titles

www.ingramcontent.com/pod-product-compliance
Lightning Source LLC
Chambersburg PA
CBHW060547060326
40690CB00017B/3630

Banana Pi Cookbook

Over 25 recipes to build projects and applications for
multiple platforms with Banana Pi

Ryad El-Dajani

PUBLISHING

BIRMINGHAM - MUMBAI

Banana Pi Cookbook

First published: June 2015

Production reference: 1240615

Published by Packt Publishing Ltd.
Livery Place
35 Livery Street
Birmingham B3 2PB, UK.

ISBN 978-1-78355-244-3

www.packtpub.com